Hermes on Two Wheels

The Sociology of Bicycle Messengers

Kevin Wehr

University Press of America,® Inc.
Lanham · Boulder · New York · Toronto · Plymouth, UK

Copyright © 2009 by
University Press of America,® Inc.
4501 Forbes Boulevard
Suite 200
Lanham, Maryland 20706
UPA Acquisitions Department (301) 459-3366

Estover Road
Plymouth PL6 7PY
United Kingdom

Library of Congress Control Number: 2009930809
ISBN-13: 978-0-7618-4793-9 (paperback : alk. paper)
ISBN-10: 0-7618-4793-6 (paperback : alk. paper)
eISBN-13: 978-0-7618-4794-6
eISBN-10: 0-7618-4794-4

Table of Contents

Preface

The many voices reproduced and analyzed in this book come from friends and fellow riders, strangers and confidants, heroes and lunatic bike punks who have shown me many things about how to live, love, and ride through life. In short, the "subjects" of this ethnographic work are not subjects at all, but people. Traditional social scientists yearn for objectivity, and thus frame their analyses in abstract and scientific language that serves to veil any bias the researcher might have. But as Weber noted almost 100 years ago, such scientific language is also a political stance. In this work, the personal *is* political *is* scientific. I use the language of social science, but I strive to never lose sight of people, politics, and place. I became a bike messenger out of a need to distract myself from the grueling work of graduate school—it was an escape from the backbiting juvenile atmosphere that can sometimes be part of academic culture. Riding allowed me to escape desks and texts, computers and advisors . . . it was also a way to make a little cash to fund my bicycle obsession. And it was a political choice as well. I am an environmentalist and I remain fully convinced that our world would be better in many ways without the massive use of fossil-fueled cars—if only we could manage a thorough reorganization of our urban space, transportation systems, and cultural constructions of "auto-nomy."

I did not start working as a courier with any intention to write an ethnographic account of bicycle messengers. My main focus of sociological research had been historical, political-economic, and environmental. But I found all of these elements came together as I began to understand the culture and occupational-structure of the messenger world. After a year or two of messengering I realized that this was not just fun and distraction, this was *data*. I realized that, in Dorothy Smith's words (1987), there was an everyday problematic here—a terrain to be explored—and I was in the perfect position to do so. I began to immerse myself in the study of participant-observation methods, the study of culture and organizations, and to look around at my fellow couriers with the open eyes of an ethnographer. I went to races and gatherings with a new attitude: I became not just a participant, but an observer as well. And so I view this work as objective not in the sense of pure science where someone in a lab coat with a clipboard looks down from some Archimedean point. Indeed there is no such omniscient point of view. Instead, this book is objective in the sense that I became a messenger: I sweated, grunted, pedaled my heart out, and carried loads so heavy that the strap on my bag snapped. I came to understand messenger culture on a deep level—deeper than any imaginary Archimedean viewer, deeper than a social science tourist who went to a few races and talked with available messengers. In short, "it takes one to know one." And even though I am now housed behind a desk and lectern in the ivory tower of academia, I still hold part of that messenger identity close to my heart. As many messengers say: "Once a messenger, always a messenger."

What I found in that new role as participant-observer was a vibrant community that was struggling in many ways. Many riders were struggling to get by financially. Some company owners were struggling to make an alternative business model work while also trying to make a life. Most were struggling with all the normal problems of life: relationships, existential angst, identity crises, and substance addictions. The community was struggling against co-optation, against the imposition of a stereotype by outsiders, corporate interests, advertisers, or poseurs. I argue that bike messengers occupy a particular space in our society, a marginal place economically and physically in the streets, and a liminal space in our culture. In this, they are like few other workers—no one else occupies the physically marginal space of the road or undergoes quite the same risks. But they are like other workers in some ways; professionals who deliver packages have similar pressures to perform, and other public service workers like the police or firefighters experience risk on a daily basis. Yet bike messengers have managed to carve out a niche free from the confines of an office job, while also managing to exist in the state-capitalist consumerist society. They unintentionally help to reproduce and maintain that society while also constructing a vibrant, rebellious, politicized subculture that has come to represent the new urban-hip, an image which coolseekers and corporate scouts have successfully, though only partially, co-opted.

After some of my research was completed, I was fortunate to participate in an academic conference session with Dorothy Smith as a discussant. The work I presented was a standard ethnography, but she pushed me to think about what she calls "institutional ethnography" (Smith 2005). This method of inquiry is a radical departure from traditional sociology, a paradigm shift of sorts. I am indebted to Smith for her insights about re-envisioning the role of the researcher and this approach to knowledge. I have come to understand my own work through this lens: to start from the thoughts and experiences of the messengers I worked with and from there move toward understanding the institutional settings of those experiences, treating those structural levels as the real objects of study. In this micro-to macro approach, I came to understand that dangerous messenger work is undertaken within the confines of the existing political-economic system, which devalues semi-skilled labor and strips people of emotional fulfillment. Voluntary risk-taking becomes a means of achieving such fulfillment as well as making a living, and cultural and stylistic expressions pay dividends in cultural scrip rather than money. A lack of financial remuneration is made up for with accrued cultural capital.

Through this process I have become indebted to many other people as well. Thanks especially to the many messengers who contributed their voices to this work, on your behalf, all the author's profits will be donated to the Bicycle Messenger Emergency Fund. Thanks also to Ben Agger, Peter Brinson, Dave Corkle, Dean Dorn, Rodney and Alice Kingsnorth, Loran Sheley, and Ellen Trescott for valuable comments and advice. And of course to FC, PB, Sparky, Jon, Burly, Shaggy, and all the others: I thank you, I miss you, I hope to see you soon for one of those long crazy rides through the wet and winding streets, chatting and laughing, blowing reds and scaring peds, cursing cabs and chasing drafts, but most importantly living and riding to the full. Without you none of this would have been worthwhile. This one is for all-y'all.

Sacramento, 2009

1. Introduction: Hermes on Two Wheels

Question: How many messengers does it take to change a light bulb?
Answer: None! Everyone knows messengers don't wait for lights to change.

I have been working for more than four years as a bicycle messenger in a Capitol city in the northern Midwest. I live on the edge of town about seven miles from the dispatch office. I wake up at 7 in the morning and ride into the central city to begin work at 8 AM. On a good day this takes 20 minutes. On the worst of days in the harsh winters it can take 40 minutes of stressful riding: being passed by SUVs splattering dirty snow-slush into my path and onto my body while I focus intently on the road, the debris, the cars, the ice, and the cracks in the pavement all at once. I ride hard to keep warm and to get there as soon as possible.

Once I meet the dispatcher and pick up the two-way radio and any immediate delivery notices, I push out again into traffic for the routine local government route. Five times a day I circle the State office buildings, picking up and dropping off packages: work orders, copies of plans, diagrams, a preliminary copy of an audit report. By weaving in and out of lanes, passing cars, cabs, and buses caught in the daily pulse of traffic, I use a small slice of the street to great effect, making government and businesses run just a bit more smoothly.

Today there is an immediate rush job. The budget process is finally complete after weeks of haggling. Now the Department of Finance has to hurry the draft budget to the government printing office, which then has to churn out dozens of copies to the legislators. The many boxes of paper will be taken back to the capitol building by truck, but it's my job to get the 100-page draft to the printing office as soon as possible.

I get the call on my cell phone from the head of the State Department of Finance. Normally a lackey summons the courier, but this is different. This is the state budget for next year, and the legislators needed it done two weeks ago. He directs me to 101 W. Wilson Street, where his main assistant will be waiting outside for me in the cold and the snow. "You can't miss her," he says, "she'll be the stressed-out one in the red overcoat who's been up all night and is nervously chain-smoking cigarettes."

I make the pick up easily enough, and weave and dodge five miles through traffic on streets slick with snow and ice, keeping pace with the cars, flying through downtown. As a bicycle messenger, I exist to make the wheels of government and commerce turn more easily, to deliver the packages and enable the state budget to be printed on time.[1] I am a human face in the anonymous bureaucracy that is our modern state. I deliver the state budget draft to the printing office, and immediately push back out into the snowy morning to pedal my way around downtown. Invisible to most, I am like the Ancient Greek messenger Hermes, but on two wheels: conveying the messages, delivering the packages, greasing the tracks of government and capitalism. Unlike Hermes with his messages from the gods, I mean business.

To most city-dwellers, bike messengers are a common part of the urban landscape: threading through traffic and flamboyantly flouting traffic laws. Many urbanites, if they even stop to ponder the question, wonder why bike messengers don't conform to social norms of behavior.[2] Why do they break the laws? Why don't they wear helmets? Why do they insist on riding so recklessly, threatening pedestrians and startling drivers? This book attempts to make sociological sense of bike messengers and show why otherwise sane people might behave in this insane manner.

Sociology, as the study of social groups and broader social structures, can offer insight into behaviors that might otherwise seem irrational. Bicycle messengers, as workers, as individuals, and as members of a dynamic subculture, offer a window into human behavior that sociology can use to further understand people generally. In this book, I will show the co-ordinating processes that link bicycle messengers in their daily lives to capitalism, representative government, and the broader culture by detailing the ways in which couriers work in a city that is designed for automobile traffic. They make creative use of physical space, but occupy a cultural position as well: the difficulties and dangers of the job require managing risk, and the low wages of the profession mean that they find repayment in other, cultural realms. Bicycle messengers embody many sociological puzzles. They work in an occupational structure that is exploitative and alienating. Their working conditions are dirty, unsafe, and unstable. They voluntarily take risks for little pay, but have developed a vibrant and visible subculture that offers other benefits. They have crafted identities within this system that are betwixt and between mainstream categories, they value authentic presentations of self, yet see others in the messenger community (though rarely themselves) at continual risk of selling out or being co-opted. Political economy, transportation structures, occupational dangers, culture, identity, liminality, authenticity, solidarity, and co-optation: There's a lot to navigate on those two wheels.

I worked as a bicycle messenger for several years and participated in the many different activities of this community: messenger races, national gatherings, Critical Mass demonstrations, and the daily grind of delivering parcels by bicycle to destinations all over the city. The voices of the messengers that give weight to this study come from hundreds of individual interviews and group conversations at gatherings of all sorts, from an international electronic discussion forum, from several published accounts of messengering, and from other sources such as newspaper articles.[3] In all cases, I have quoted messengers exactly, without editing for grammar, spelling, or punctuation; all use of slang, spelling or grammatical errors, and obscenities originate with the person quoted.[4] While sometimes difficult to read, the quotations contained in this study will hopefully give the reader a more precise understanding of messenger style and approach to communication, and thus their feelings about their experiences.

Municipal transportation systems cater to car traffic at the expense of bicycle traffic. Some cities have special bike lanes, and others even have traffic signals for bikes. But in most cities, cycling is not an easy method of transportation. It is either actively chosen (perhaps due to political orientation), or it is passively accepted (generally by those economically marginalized groups who have few other choices, such as students or children). Messengers straddle these two categories of active choice versus passive acceptance. For many couriers, it is an "outside job," free from office-building cubicles and out from under the watchful eye of the boss. For some it is a place where they can dress how they please, behave as they care to, and avoid the strict confines of many workplaces. For the majority of messengers, however, it is just a way to make rent—more or less like any other, though risky and dirty, with low pay and few benefits. For these messengers it is a relatively unskilled position that requires little, outside of physical effort. Like popping rivets on an assembly line or bagging groceries at the supermarket, messengering can sometimes be "just another job."

Bicycle messengering thus attracts people from many different parts of society—some do it for the love of the bike, some do it as a political statement, and some do it because it is slightly less distasteful than the available alternatives. Though some of them desire to live outside mainstream capitalist society in stylish subcultural rebellion, all bicycle messengers actually help to maintain and reproduce capitalism and representational government by moving packages smoothly through the city.

Why do they do it? To the casual observer, messengers may seem like lunatics on wheels. They are often represented in popular culture as the anti-hero of the urban jungle: the dirty, smelly recurring figures in movies and commercials symbolizing the dark underside and accelerated pace of the city. Yet the vast majority of messengers are not like this at all. Most cycle couriers are just workers who use the entire street, stretching space to accommodate the needs of the moment. Couriers generally ride between auto traffic and parked cars, but are sometimes forced to dart into traffic to avoid carelessly opened car doors or other hazards. To get packages to clients on time, messengers ride in between traffic lanes, occasionally on sidewalks, and sometimes the wrong way down one-way streets. When traffic gets bad in the city, especially when gridlock approaches, this elastic space becomes a niche for bicycle couriers. The perfect illustration of this was the ability of bike messengers to move information and materials around lower Manhattan immediately following the tragic events of the morning of 11 September 2001. When the streets were closed and chaos reigned, many messengers volunteered their time to help move food, water, and medical supplies around the area surrounding "ground zero."

If it seems that messengers ride like lunatics, they do so largely because they have to: couriers carry any number of documents or packages from one office building to another. They are generally paid on a piece rate, so the more quickly they deliver each single piece (or "tag" or "run"), the more they can carry in a day, and the more cash they ride home with each week. This is encouraged and even required by dispatchers, delivery companies, and the clients themselves. If a tag is not delivered promptly, or if a rush delivery (a "rush" or "hot shot") doesn't arrive across town in the promised time frame (sometimes ten minutes or less) then the courier may not be paid at all. The structure of the delivery industry marginalizes messengers with low pay and slight job security and almost never provides any health insurance or other benefits. Like all of us, couriers work within a competitive capitalist system, and the occupational structure is defined in part by the larger political-economic system and in part by decisions made by individual messenger companies.

Social institutions are the stable, salient facts of life that govern much of our behavior, even if they are invisible. Who can point to the social structure of the economy? There are agencies, policies, and specific locations where social institutions find concrete instantiation—Wall Street, the US Treasury, or the cash register at the corner market. But the larger social structure of the economy is bigger than all of this, and such social institutions define the unwritten rules that govern our actions, ideals, goals, and even some of our thoughts. In a capitalist economy, for instance, competition and financial risk are rewarded, producing a set of cultural behaviors that valorize aggressive individual action. Many people believe in these values without question, indeed many consider it to be a natural state of affairs. But this is not the only way that an economy could influence individual behavior—in fact, non-capitalist economies produce radically non-competitive behaviors of mutual co-operation (think of historical Native American society, or the contemporary examples of worker collectives), thus showing that different structures condition different ideas of what is natural. The economy is one such structure, the political realm is another, and individuals may have different responses to these structures—in fact people through our daily actions help to produce and reproduce these structures.

But those reproductions and responses are also predictable in many ways. We live within social structures of racism and patriarchy as well as democracy and capitalism, and these structures produce identifiable social-psychological responses. We seek security, stability, and fulfillment, sometimes by making use of social structures, and sometimes by pushing against them. In our everyday actions we help to create and recreate those social structures—when we go to work, when we buy our groceries, when we pay our rent. Peter Berger (1963) has used the analogy of acrobats on stage to illustrate how we reproduce social structures: with great agility and athleticism we all balance against one another, building a human pyramid of action that reinforces itself over time, day-in and day-out. Social institutions exert great power over individual behavior, both enabling certain freedoms, but also constraining many activities and ideas. Charles Lemert has called these "social things," facts on the ground that carry great social weight and produce and reproduce norms of action and understandings about the world (Lemert 2005). Chapters 2 and 3 show how the broader social context and the structure of the bike messenger industry push riders to engage in the risky behaviors that cause consternation to many city dwellers.

These couriers, flying around the city, delivering packages, have formed a distinctive culture based around common experiences. Many messengers congregate at slow times of the day, after work, and on weekends. They race against one another in friendly competition. They support each other in their city and around the globe through mutual assistance associations. They gather at annual events that are part race, part party, and part carnival. And they have organized associations to improve working conditions and help deal with the onslaught of media attention (both positive and negative) that has helped to make messengers a gritty symbol of the downtown core. The structure of the industry puts a premium on speed, and messenger culture valorizes this requirement by honoring skill and the embrace of risk. But the culture is also focused on mutual aid, fun, play, and politics. These creative and colorful individuals constitute what one courier called "the last non co-opted punk subculture." Of course, much of this subculture has been co-opted in recent years.

But these distinctive and stylish messengers so visibly flaunting traffic laws, with their unusual and distinctive style that is so often used by cultural entrepreneurs, actually represent a minority of bike couriers. The flashy kid on a track bike[5] blazing through traffic might be a messenger, but could just as easily be on his way to the library at the University, or the patio of the local coffee shop, late for his latté. The vast majority of bike messengers—perhaps 85 percent—do not dress in distinctive garb, ride clunky mountain bikes, and don't participate in the broader messenger community. Why the difference? Why do some messengers adopt a particular cultural style, while others don't seem to care? Why would anyone, under such working conditions, embrace the job to such an extent that they appear to be on the job even when they are not? This book attempts to answer this quandary by analyzing different types of bicycle messengers to see how they respond differently to similar social pressures. Sociology can help us to understand how comparably situated individuals may react in very different manners, and may assign quite disparate meanings to the same circumstances.

Bicycle messengers occupy a complex position in the city and in our culture: they are somewhere in between cars and pedestrians, they operate at the margins of the street, and their jobs pay the low wages common to the service sector. They are somewhere in between, or *liminal*: not quite one, and yet not exactly the other (Turner 1967). Yet this status of being liminal—being different from others—is precisely what binds this unique community together: through rituals of working, racing, and partying, messengers build and rebuild their community, in many cases taking pride in their difference. Pierre Bourdieu has written extensively on the production and reproduction of culture in contemporary society: Communities can be formed by tradition, through common experiences of adversity, or because of similarities in experience. These connections can be fleeting, or even imaginary, but often they are persistent, even if they are informal (Anderson 1991). There are cultural symbols that stand out too—some people find spatial and cultural meaning in postal zip codes (Beverly Hills 90210) or telephone area codes (Brooklyn 718), people identify with a place, a group, an occupation, or a style of self-presentation. Cultural communities are developed in part by individuals practicing improvisational techniques within the larger structures of society, something Bourdieu called the *habitus* (Bourdieu 1977, 1984).

Messengers, too, produce and reproduce a unique cultural community that attracts many outsiders to the industry, including advertising executives, movie producers, and everyday people searching for authenticity. Messengers are increasingly visible as symbols of an accelerated urban life. As messengers gain a more prominent place in the popular consciousness, they also become subject to the possibility of co-optation. Chapters 4 and 5 discuss risk and culture in the dynamics of the bicycle messenger community, and show how messengers navigate the issues of dangerous streets, cultural co-optation, and other community matters, particularly the pitfalls and rewards of "selling out."

Bike messengers are conspicuous symbols of urban life. As with many symbols, we see ourselves reflected in them. We may covet their ability to beat traffic during gridlock, we may envy their distinctive style, or we may admire their courage in the face of great risk. But what attracts us to bike messengers is not just the way they beat traffic while remaining calm, cool, and collected—what makes them stand out is the way they navigate the vagaries of modern life. Robert Bellah and colleagues (1985) argued that one of the issues that we face today is the balance of individualism and commitment—Americans are promised the pursuit of happiness, but too often we can't seem to attain it and we find ourselves isolated, yearning for a lost sense of community. Much earlier, Karl Marx noticed this isolation in the labor process (1967 [1867]), and called it *alienation*. Max Weber saw something similar in the increase of rationalization in society, and called it *disenchantment* (1946 [1913]). Emile Durkheim, in studying the modernization process, noticed that the pace of behavioral change could outpace the development of new norms, a phenomenon he called *anomie* (1984 [1893]).[6] These early sociologists, though coming from different perspectives and not speaking about identical issues, all noticed that it seemed as if people were missing something in their lives—there is some gap to be filled, a lacunae between our everyday experience and what we hope for. Some modern theorists have called this a malaise of the postmodern condition (Lyotard 1979). David Harvey (1989) and other theorists suggest that this is an issue of late- or hyper-capitalism. These different takes on the present moment all suggest that, regardless of terminology, people feel as if something new and different is going on, something that involves a loss of tradition and authentic identity, a diminution of culture, or the savagery of the economy. This book argues that bike messengers are objects of fascination in part because they have crafted an identity and a culture that offers excitement and authenticity in a society increasingly characterized by ennui and normalcy. They belong to a supportive community, which has evolved over the last 20 years, and which insulates them from the alienation of capitalism and modern society. They have solved some of the riddles of modern existence, and have done so without selling out their ideals. Even if they seem like lunatics on two wheels to the rest of us, they know better.

This book focuses on a specific group within the larger society, and attempts to clarify the diversity of courier perspectives and the dynamics of messenger culture, but it is also a comment on the modern moment that we all live in. The accelerating pace of life produces swirling identities and shifting meanings, causing many to crave stronger roots, a feeling of belonging, or an expression of solidarity. The desire for community can be seen in real estate trends like "new urbanism," which provide neighborhoods that are more conducive to community building than the commuter suburbs that so many Americans currently live in. The search for "realness" is manifested in the advertising world's "coolseekers," who comb the streets of Brooklyn or San Francisco for the next hip urban fad, to be ironically mass-marketed to those of us not lucky enough to live in a cultural capitol. We can see it in the drive towards "extreme sports," where people push the envelope in search of exhilaration that can offset the drudgery of an office job in a cubicle. And we can see it in the mimicry of young people as they model themselves after the style, behavior and attitudes of others. Finding one's niche has often been a struggle, and contemporary society is no exception. In fact, technological change offers those who wander the Internet many new blogscapes to explore and modes of identity to try out. New forms of community are multiplying, and many of us are overwhelmed and paralyzed by the array before us.

When faced with such a wide variety of choices, it is easy to fall prey to a naïve relativism, where any culture is available for co-optation or mimicry, and any choice seems as valid as any other. In this moment, sometimes referred to as "postmodern," we can access news and information from around the world, co-sponsored by this-or-that megacorporation. Commodities are assembled from parts crafted in sweatshop factories in several different nations of the global South, then marketed and sold to first-world consumers at premium prices. Every television channel seems to report the same celebrity spectacle in mind-numbing minutia, but news that really connects to our everyday lives can be hard to come by. In response, we get bloggers and independent media activists who purport to offer us "real" news or "on the ground" information. We see the rise of "handcrafted" indigenous products offered in place of homogenous plasticized trinkets. People move from the identical houses of the suburbs into the gentrified city core, or to planned developments whose marketing references some lost, imaginary "Leave it to Beaver" time when community was more prevalent. This searching suggests a suspicion about the "official version" and a craving for authenticity. Sociology, can move between examining micro levels of individual issues and macro levels of social problems. The trick is to connect these two levels using what C. Wright Mills called the *sociological imagination* (Mills 1959). Bicycle messengers may represent a small subcultural group, but in certain ways they have solved some of these broader social problems of alienation, ennui, and the search for meaning and authenticity. And messengers would appear to offer something of a solution to these urges for those who would mimic them. This book explores those solutions and how others have responded. It is a sociological examination of bike messengers, but it is also about all of us.

Notes

1. This is an example of what Dorothy Smith (1987) calls an everyday problematic: a terrain that bears exploration and discussion. We often view the state as some cold, antiseptic, juggernaut of bureaucracy, with gears that grind on, no matter what. But in fact the state is made up of people acting out their daily lives. Legislators that debate a state budget, their staff who write it up in formal language according to rules about procedure, and the messengers who deliver it to the printing office. These everyday actions, according to Smith (2005), are the ruling relations that are created through our actions, which co-ordinate both our local actions and those of people across the state, to whom us busy worker-bees are truly anonymous.

2. Social norms—those co-ordinated behaviors that come to us so immediately—are in fact produced by our own daily actions, and then continue to co-ordinate our practices over time. They are rigid in some ways, being salient and durable over time. But they are malleable, too, and can change over time as our daily behaviors evolve and people begin to get comfortable with different ways of living.

3. See the Methodological Appendix for more detail.

4. To maintain tone, style, and presentation, the normal editorial insertion of [*sic*] will not be practiced. To ensure confidentiality no real names are given (easily identifiable nicknames are also changed) except for those from published sources.

5. The track bike has a single gear and often no brakes. Pedaled forward the bike will go forward, pedaled backwards the bike will go backwards. Those who ride without brakes apply reverse pressure on the pedals to slow down, or stand on the pedals to halt the rear wheel completely and skid to a stop. This type of bicycle was developed for velodrome track racing, hence the name "track bike." Since the single rear cog is fixed in place, it is also known as a "fixed gear" or a "fixie." As discussed in Chapter 4, this type of bicycle has become a strong symbol of messenger culture.

6. Of course these terms are not synonyms. While Marx was discussing the consequences of the capitalist wage-labor system, Durkheim was responding to accelerating shifts in social norms, and Weber noted the increasing rationalization of modern life. Though these three classical theorists were clearly talking about distinct concepts in different contexts arising from different causal processes, it is worthy to note that each concept involves loss, strain, or non-authenticity, and each implies a search for a more fulfilling life.

2. Why Does Hermes Fly?

"It's russian roulette everyday."[1]

Bike messengers represent the urban hipster: stylish, sophisticated, individualistic, speeding through town, rising above the traffic congestion, doing their own thing. But many people know little more about couriers than what they see as the rider flies by, squeezed between cars on his way to another drop-off location. This chapter will describe the organization of the occupation—its opportunities and constrictions—to give a foundation for the subsequent examination of risk, culture, and the community of messengers.

The structure of work: old school solutions to new school capitalism

There are messengers in almost every major city around the world. Though this book focuses primarily on North American couriers, there are working messengers in Japan, China, and India, in Mexico City and Guatemala City, and in even minor cities across Europe. Messengers may (rarely) ride $3000 hand-crafted bikes, but quite often they push $20 clunkers around town—bikes that probably wouldn't be stolen even if they were not locked up. Each city's messengers may have their own distinctions, but the same basic organization of work is evident everywhere.

Speedy package delivery is entirely the point of messengering. Messenger culture has plenty of splash, class, and panache, but its fundamental reason for being is to move materials from one place to another. Individual messengers are connected via radio or cell phone to a central dispatcher. Clients call in pick-up/delivery requests (a "run" or a "job"), the dispatcher writes this up (a "tag") and relays the information to a messenger, who compiles the information on a manifest sheet. The messenger goes to the pick-up location, notes the time of pick up and the delivery address, and then proceeds to the delivery location, getting the manifest sheet signed at the drop-off point as proof of delivery. They may carry blueprints from an architecture firm, court filings from a law office, or promotional materials from an advertising firm. But mostly they carry mystery objects—manila envelopes or brown paper packages that carry no meaning to the courier other than weight, dimension, and distance carried.[2] The messenger is paid for the number of deliveries completed each day (with rushes or long distance runs sometimes paid more, depending on the fee structure of the particular firm). Just like the typical cab driver, a messenger is thus dependent on the dispatcher to assign the choice runs—much grumbling is heard about inequities perpetuated by dispatchers who sometimes favor a particular messenger (or gender, or race, or who are biased against neophytes). Bicycle messengers employ a decidedly nineteenth-century technology to solve some of the most basic problems of capitalism: how to get bits of physical information from one location to another as fast as possible.

Bike messenger companies operate within the capitalist system in a classic competitive manner. Messengers are subject to the pressures of capitalism just as we all are. Though many of the mechanisms of capitalism are so familiar to us that they seem almost invisible or inevitable, capitalism works in some very specific ways and has predictable outcomes. As Marx and his many followers have shown, capitalism is predicated on several foundational principles (Marx 1967 [1867]). The first is private property: individual capitalists must legally own the means of production to be assured of recouping investment. This means that the state (broadly understood) must secure the right of ownership and offer mechanisms of enforcement (the courts, the police, etc.). Under capitalism, wage labor is both a means of production that the worker "owns" and also an input commodity for the capitalist production process. Workers must be free in two ways: they are *free from* slavery and *free to* sell their labor on the open market. This freedom, however, is illusory since workers must sell their labor or face starvation.

In the capital production process the owner starts with money that he invests in productive material (a factory, land for agriculture, etc) and hires workers to run the process. The resulting commodities are then sold on the market for money. This process, then, means that money is transformed into a commodity through labor, and then into new money. The amount that a capitalist ends with after paying costs must be more than what they started with. If it is not, the process fails. If the capitalist's money is increased, it is known as profit.

Where does profit come from? One school of thought says that it comes from the capitalist's investment risk and the work of organizing the production process. Another school of thought suggests that without the labor of the workers, no profit could be realized. Capitalists and laborers are inter-dependent in the production process; without both sides acting in good faith, the process stalls.

If we fix the costs of other parts of the system, then we can see that profit is the difference between the amount paid to the laborer and the amount of value produced by the laborer. If profit is determined at least in part by the cost of labor, rational profit-driven capitalists will adopt technology into the production process if it helps reduce labor costs, improves turnover time, or otherwise confers a special advantage to the producer. Since all capitalists will strive to gain this advantage, competition to adopt technology contributes to the tendency of the rate of profit to fall. Falling profit, in turn, produces crisis that, Marx argues, is inherently embedded in the system (Marx 1967 [1867]).

There are two difficulties at the core of Marx's analysis of capitalism. Profit comes from the increased value of a commodity, value that is added by labor. This means that profit is created socially in the production process. But capitalists take this profit as reward for their risk. To Marx, this social production but private appropriation of profit represents a contradiction. Capitalists have an interest in maximizing their profit, and so will adopt technology or otherwise attempt to pay as few costs as they can, including the lowest wages possible. Over time this downward pressure on wages means that workers are pushed to the margins of subsistence. When workers can no longer afford to buy the things they need, commodities are left on the shelves. If the goods are not bought, capitalists can't realize their profit and the system stalls. Marx called this an overproduction crisis: too many goods are produced and not enough are consumed.

This contradiction is at the center of many contemporary political battles, though it is not always clear what is at stake. Debates about fixing a federal minimum wage address this question while not obviously seeming to. A larger minimum wage means less profit for capitalists, but the workers have more ability to buy commodities. In the face of an economic crisis, the state can sometimes act to make capitalism run more smoothly. In the 1930s the federal government created a social security program, in more recent times a helping hand was offered in the form of food stamps. This safety net function is the basis for a great deal of legitimacy for most modern nation-states for the voting public. Imagine if the elderly were starving, or if wages were so low that masses of people couldn't pay rent or afford food. People wouldn't stand for it, and the risk of revolt against those in power would increase. The more miserable people are, or so the argument goes, the more likely they would be to see through the veil to understand their own true interest in social revolution.[3]

But if there is a downward pressure on wages (to the floor established by law or the market), then why do people feel like they are doing better now than they were before? This is a complex cultural question about why people think the way they do, and it's not easy to get inside people's heads. What can be said is that regardless of their beliefs, people on average are not doing as well as they were a generation ago, especially at the poorer end of the wage scale. Even though we have ipods and cell phones and video games, the take-home pay for most workers in the last 30 years has remained stagnant while the costs of living have gone up. Several things have happened to make it seem like we are not living in difficult economic times. First, the invention of credit 100 years ago allowed the working class to purchase goods now and pay for them later. This meant more flexibility in consumption and workers could "fake it till they make it." Second, women entered the workforce *en masse* after World War II, providing a second income for many households. The resulting increased family income allowed greater consumption for the first 20 years after World War II, but in the last 30 years adjusted wages have not kept up with inflation (Bureau of Labor Statistics 2007, Boskin et al 1998, Hausman 1999, Hobsbawm 1996a, Hobsbawm 1996b, Levy and Temin 2007, Schumpeter 1934, Scott and Tilly 1989, Shapiro and Greenstein 1997, Vidal and Zeidenberg 2007).

An example might be useful. In 1960 in Sacramento, California (the Capitol of the State) an average home cost about $60,000. A generation later, an analogous house cost about $450,000. Meanwhile, the median wage moved from $20,000 to about $50,000. The ratio of housing cost to median income in 1960 was about 3:1, today it is 9:1. The costs of living, especially housing, have gone up dramatically, but wages have not risen as sharply, meaning that home-ownership is now largely out of reach for an increasing amount of the population, at least in Sacramento. Most bicycle messengers earn substantially less than the median income, and home-ownership is generally out of the question.

This basic analysis of capitalism was identified by Karl Marx 150 years ago. Some things about it have not changed at all, but other things have changed drastically. Social analysts offer several ideas for understanding these changes: accelerated capitalism, fast capitalism, hyper capitalism, post-Fordism, and postmodernism to name a few. These concepts have important differences, but all of them recognize that things move faster today than they did 150 years ago. Without entering the complex debate over terminology, I will use the term "fast capitalism" to indicate the acceleration of the present moment. The turnover rate (from money, to commodities, to more money), the recouping of profits, technology adoption, and information exchange are all moving at an increasing speed. While this phenomenon is well established in many parts of the world, developing nations and regions may exhibit uneven tendencies. What is not always recognized, however, is the uneven development within the so-called advanced economies. Social change is rarely a uni-linear process, and technology within fast capitalism is no different. This is one way to begin to understand why bike messengers still crisscross our cities.

The ubiquitous use of technology invented in the nineteenth century (the bicycle) to carry information that could otherwise be transferred in micro-moments via the (increasingly wireless) information network seems counter-intuitive. The fact that a guy on a bike can get something across the downtown core faster and more cheaply than any alternative shows that some sectors of fast capitalism must still rely on comparatively "slow" technologies, even with the advent of personal computers and the transfer of information by email, fax machine, and the Internet.

The rapid adoption of new technology has characterized capitalism from the beginning, but in the current moment of fast capitalism, this pace has increased. We adopt new technologies and come to rely on them very quickly; each new gadget builds upon older technology that we come to take for granted. We multi-task overlapping jobs: I google-up answers for vaguely phrased questions on a laptop, while reading email, and using a cell phone to communicate with friends, the boss, my family. Each succeeding generation cannot imagine life without the new tools, but each new tool is based on inventions of the past: the Internet started by using telephone lines, which in turn was based on the telegraph. And so our progress stands upon previous innovations.

We easily accept technology into our lives, but these devices have not managed to displace some fundamental needs. Handwritten signatures on original hard copy documents remain a legal requirement. Printed copies passed hand-to-hand are still the standard in many industries. Blueprints and graphic design file sizes are often too large to be processed via standard Internet technology—and too precious to trust to the post. Videos, DVDs, and promotional items all get carried by bike messengers, as does the dossier that a corporate bigwig forgot at his last meeting across the financial district. I once got a call to pick up a pair of prescription sunglasses that a real estate developer had forgotten, and another time I was hired to ride to a liquor store, pick up a pre-paid bottle of expensive scotch, and deliver it across town as a year-end gift from an appreciative out-of-town client. The delivery industry handles these anti-technological remnants regardless of high-speed data transmission.

Technology has changed the messenger industry as well. New metal alloys and carbon-fiber technology have made bicycles lighter than ever before, though you might not know it by looking at some beat-up messenger bikes. The trials of a bike messenger's day have further eased with the introduction of two-way radios, cell phones, and other communication devices. Instead of going back and forth between the dispatch office and individual delivery addresses as happened for much of the twentieth century, in the 1980s messengers began to carry a pager and would stop at pay phones to get details on the next delivery. Today a messenger can speak with their dispatcher directly while riding through the downtown by using wireless technology. Most messengers borrow either a cell phone or a two-way radio from the delivery company every morning. They strap it to their messenger bag for easy access while negotiating traffic: one hand on the handlebars and one hand on the radio. Messengers sometimes make use of the standard CB codes of 10-4 (yes, affirmative), 10-20 (what is your location), etc. More usually, couriers in a company or a city develop informal rules. Creative and colorful radio traffic is common, but certain patterns and code words get ingrained. To this day when I hear a certain cell phone ring-tone I have to stop myself from jumping to go make a pick-up.

Aside from technological innovations, in some ways not much about capitalism has fundamentally changed in the late term—after all, labor power is still exploited for the profit of the owner, and without the extension of the credit industry and the entry of women into the labor market, crisis might have erupted much sooner. But not much has changed in the delivery business. Bike messengers are classic service industry workers: They pick up a package, transport it across town, and deliver it within a certain time frame. For this, clients pay a price. Some amount of this is paid to the delivery person with the rest going to overhead, advertising, and to support management and the profits of the company. Bike messengers are generally paid on a piece-rate system—a fixed amount per package and by distance. Thus, the faster the courier rides, the more they are paid. The company where I worked used this structure so that within the downtown core I was paid about $2.00 for each package delivered. The company charged several times this cost to the customer. There were two concentric rings, beyond which the cost of the delivery went up with the riding time, $5.00 for a medium (5-10 mile) ride, and $7.00 for anything over 10 miles. The faster that I could ride those miles, the more money I could realize per hour. Any minute of rest, any moment without a package in my bag meant that I was not making money.

Rush jobs can pay even more, and long rush jobs can be lucrative. But the risks can be high, as in one example where I was assigned a rush job. I had to go out five miles from downtown to make a pick up, and return downtown to make the drop off—a ten mile round trip, and I had just 30 minutes to do it. Riding steadily that would mean averaging almost 20 miles per hour the whole time. There's no waiting for red lights at a time like this. So I'm coming across a major thoroughfare and I see that if I ride hard I can catch the end of the green light, so I sprint through it, getting up to perhaps 30 mph, forgetting that down the block is a railroad crossing. As I came up to the tracks I was faced with a choice: I could either slow down and lose precious moments, or I could try to lift my bike and jump the tracks in what is known as a bunny hop. I chose the latter, but I didn't make it. My rear wheel caught the far edge of the raised lip of pavement and I got a flat tire known as a "snakebite."[4] I made the wrong choice, and instead of losing moments from slowing down, I lost minutes to changing a tire. I walked my bike two lucky blocks to a bike shop to use their high-pressure air hose and changed the tube. Rather than two small punctures, the speed I was going had ripped two parallel gashes and dented the wheel. I made the repair, pushed off into traffic again, and somehow made the delivery in time. Due to my rash decision, the cost of a new tube meant that my $10.00 pay went down to $7.00 for 30 minutes of hard work.

In this context, classic incentive structures encourage workers to perform their tasks as quickly—but as carefully—as possible: Just as the migrant laborer is paid per bushel that they pick, the faster the messenger completes each task, the higher the daily wage. The company still enjoys the fruits of the cyclist's labor, and the structure of the occupation assists in the perpetuation of the capitalist system through the efficient transferring of information across town (Riley 2000; Cully 2001).

The organization of work in the short-distance delivery industry marginalizes couriers beyond the standard exploitative relationship of owner to worker. In typical fashion for a capitalist system, it is those who actually get the work done—those most crucial to the process—who undertake the greatest physical risk but receive the least reward. The pay is low, the danger is high, and job security and health care are nearly non-existent. But couriers continue to ride, and ride as fast as they can. The piece-rate system puts a premium on knowing the ins and outs of the city, the ways to work around traffic, the secret routes, where the back-doors are, and other tidbits of information that come with time and experience. This specialized knowledge is built over time as a courier learns the city and the peculiarities of the addresses. The development of this knowledge shows how messengering de-centers the notion of skilled vs. unskilled labor. Bike couriers are not like ditch diggers, nor are they like auto mechanics. They have a certain set of skills, and much of what sets fast messengers apart from slower ones is their mental map of the city and its buildings. The working class pride that many couriers take in knowing all the tricks to move quickly through the city is a reflection of the structure of the piece-rate system.

Usually the piece-rate system doesn't add up to much over the workweek, but occasionally just the right constellation of events comes together to make a great day. There was one spring day that brought steady calls from remote locations with easy pick-up and drop-off routes. This happily combined with a set of special deliveries that I could work into the normal daily deliveries. Over the long day's work I actually made almost enough money to pay a full month's rent (though I was living very cheaply at the time in shared housing). This, however, was rare; most days the total tags added up to "never enough." But the faster a courier rides, the more money they make, so the piece-rate system thus encourages couriers to ride as fast as possible, to take risks, and to engage in the reckless behavior that couriers are known for (discussed in depth in Chapter 3). This is required by the dispatchers, the delivery companies, and the clients themselves: if a tag is not delivered promptly, or if a rush job doesn't arrive across town in the promised time frame, the courier may not be paid for the work at all.

So while messengers are subject to the standard capitalist process of exploitation, in some ways they move against this current. Wage work in a capitalist system has the character of alienation: labor is exchanged for a fixed wage during commodity production. This commodity is sold on the market for more than the wage and costs of production, yielding a surplus value known as profit. The commodity that the workers produce is more valuable than the wage they are paid, yet they get nothing more than the promised wage—some call this fair, others exploitation. And workers are divorced from the product of their labor since the commodity is sold impersonally on the market (what Marx called alienation). As consumers we go shopping at Wal-Mart and see products, prices, discounts, or package deals. We do not usually see these things as the result of a labor process; we aren't cognizant of the human energy that is embodied in the goods on the shelves. We almost certainly don't think about the meager wages paid to third world laborers in order to give us those cheap prices we have come to depend on. The service industry is similar, but more immediate. At the drive-in fast food restaurant we order through a microphone from some invisible worker, and consume a burger wrapped to look just like every other one that comes off the line. We know, on some level, that someone cooked the burger, salted the fries, and filled the soda cup. And we see someone at the end of the line put it all in a bag and take our money. But we rarely think of the humanity in this process. We don't think of our fast food meal as the result of a labor process; we just think of it as satisfying the need we have for sustenance. But it *is* the end of a process, one that stretches further back than many care to think about. There is much labor outside of the immediacy of our experience. Farmers had to grow the wheat, which had to be milled into flour, and a baker had to process this and other material just so that the hamburger bun could get to your lunch table. This is an iterative process for the meat, the special sauce, the lettuce, the cheese, and it repeats for all the millions served in the fast food chains.

Messengering is a classic service industry in this vein, but bike couriers have more latitude than their counterparts in other service sectors. They have a supervisor (the dispatcher), but they operate on their own outside of physical scrutiny as they ride around the city. They are connected via two-way radio, but this is a relatively weak supervision mechanism compared with a direct oversight on the shop floor or camera surveillance over the cash register in many work places. Messengers also have more direct contact with clients in face-to-face deliveries as compared with many service workers. Unlike the fast-food burger that is cooked by one person, assembled by another, and served by a third, the courier streaking across town is the same worker who carries the package upstairs and gets the signature from the secretary. When the delivery is made quickly, the courier can get praise directly from a client (and when they're late, they know that right away too). As one courier in Spain told me, "as a messenger, I have always felt a little less divorced from my labor. I have considerably more responsibility than someone on an assembly line." Like some other occupations—mechanics and construction workers come to mind—messengers have a quality of working class pride and a certain code of ethics that reflect this level of responsibility.

Any courier can inflict damage on their employer or their clients, and generally they take this responsibility seriously. The same courier in Spain said: "Do messengers have some sort of code of honor not to touch the shit that they're carrying? I do, even when I'm working for a company that I hate." Couriers know that they can hurt the clients or delivery company, and they know that the materials they carry are valuable—sometimes even irreplaceable. One long-time fixture in the Minneapolis courier community produced a sew-on patch for messenger bags that reads "Your career is in my bag. How much is it worth?" Imagine if those court papers were not filed on time, or if the blueprints arrived at the construction site wet from the rain. The reputation of the lawyers and architects literally is carried in the messenger's bag, and this exemplifies the double edge of exploitation: the worker needs the boss to organize the workplace, but the boss needs the worker to get the job done and the client needs the work performed at a high level of quality. Messengers not only have a dispatcher or supervisor, they also have direct communication with the client, the end-consumer of their services. The Minneapolis courier's patch underscores the importance and value of the messenger's labor.

Though bike couriers are at the mercy of the dispatcher for plum jobs, they might also take advantage of the lack of direct supervision to maximize their income. Some messengers will "call in empty" indicating that they have completed all their deliveries even though in fact they have not. This allows them to set up a series of pick ups and drop offs and carry more packages at once, increasing total deliveries, and thus maximizing their paycheck (it also makes them seem quicker than they actually are in the eyes of the dispatcher). Indeed, some savvy messengers will play a high-stakes game of moonlighting by secretly setting up their own independent company, or even working for two companies at once. With two-way radio technology this is easy enough to do, though it can make for some stressful periods under high demand, or if a few longer deliveries come through at the same time. Thus, messengers work within the ruling relations of the piece-rate system, but they have learned ways to resist the dictates of those with power. Such little rebellions are what make the difference between a normal and a lucrative day for a messenger.

When messengers manipulate the system by playing this "trick the dispatcher" game it puts individual messengers in competition with each other. Messengers know that they are indispensable to their clients as a category, even though any one individual courier may be interchangeable with the next. In principle this could give couriers a great deal of group-based power. The classic labor-management power dynamic gives the privilege to hire and fire to the boss, but workers are indispensable to the process and can slow down or stop work to inflict economic harm to the bosses. This system is normally kept in balance by both sides co-operating.

Bike messengers in most cities, however, do not currently have the necessary solidarity to act as a self-interested economic unit. Though they offer a crucial service as a group, each courier could be easily replaced by one of the legions of willing cyclists (discussed in Chapter 5). The many young men who would jump at the chance for a messenger job are an example of a "reserve labor force" in capitalism. Those who are seeking work put a downward pressure on wages, for those with a job cannot demand higher wages if there are people willing to take that job for low pay. The reserve army of labor also serves a social control function, keeping current employees in line and following the rules: it forces co-operation. A large reserve of labor enables a competitive market for wages, and breeds competition on the job as well. The threat of replacement, the competition for good runs to maximize their low pay, and the pride in doing their job quickly and efficiently are all barriers that keep couriers from organizing around their mutual interests. The structure of the industry raises this barrier even higher.

Though clients assume that messengers are employees of a delivery company, this status is actually quite unstable. Most messengers are categorized as "Independent Contractors" (or ICs) who are paid per delivery with no fixed contract. They can show up for work one day and skip the next (though this behavior generally earns one a bad reputation). Couriers often can work their own schedule: for 6 hours or 12, taking a delivery offered by the dispatcher or, quite rarely, not accepting it. They often have to provide their own bike, their own bag, their own helmet, and their own insurance and bonding. This setup is accepted (and even embraced by some) despite significant disadvantages to the couriers. Many couriers value not having a fixed schedule, which allows them to live an alternative lifestyle. Others decry IC status as akin to indentured labor. Using an IC structure means that courier companies can operate with what is called flexible accumulation: there is no job security, no health care or other benefits, and no need to provide protections like those afforded to other delivery professionals, such as bonding or insurance.

A delivery truck driver in a uniform is granted some level of respect, or perceived professionalism. But bike messengers often are not granted the same courtesies. As one courier put it:

> well, i was told at this one building that i had to leave my bag. in a wooden box. on the dock. which was open, so basically they were telling me i had to leave my bag. unattended. in the alley. fedex, ups, any old yahoo walking-in in a suit could be carrying any manner of package or luggage and they don't get so much as a second glance.

Because of the perception of messengers as unprofessional, a perception that is reproduced through the IC status (not to mention sweaty clothing) they are forced to the economic margins of the system. IC status reinforces the individualizing tendencies produced by the piece-rate system, competition for good runs, and a large army of reserve labor.

The structure of this system guarantees that the faster a rider is, the more money he will get paid (assuming he's favored by the dispatcher!). This is why a premium is put on speed, agility, and creative approaches to beating traffic. Dispatchers and managers tend to "look the other way" when it comes to such creativity, as it generally involves illegality. Messengers will run red lights and stop signs, weave in and out of lanes of traffic, use the sidewalk, median strips, and even ride into on-coming traffic or the wrong way down a one-way street in order to get a package to a client just a little bit faster. Such risky behavior is required by the structure of the system, is tacitly encouraged by the dispatchers and clients, and is valorized in messenger culture. As one courier put it: "It ain't the job, it's the jobsite! It's not the work, but the workplace!!" And in fact the workplace—the streets—are full of obstacles that slow down a messenger. Red lights are easily ignored once a messenger learns how to navigate cross-traffic: you simply weave your way through. Pedestrians are another matter entirely, as they often pay little attention to their surroundings. As one Dublin messenger said, in discussing the challenges of an old city with narrow streets:

> the streets aren't too wide so people feel they can make it across pretty easily, therefore they hurl themselves in front of you, lemming-like.

Avoiding wandering pedestrians, flouting traffic laws, using all parts of the street, messengers engage in risky behaviors simply as part of the job. Though this risk is not necessarily highly remunerated, it is a point of pride for many messengers, just as risk-taking behaviors are differently valued in many dangerous (and typically masculine) professions, as will be discussed in Chapter 4 (Lois 2003; Lyng 1990).

Many argue that these antics contribute to a negative public perception of messengers. Daredevil behavior does not always earn the label of "hero." While clients and dispatchers may appreciate a rider who is skilled in creative approaches to traffic, many drivers and pedestrians see such riders as maniacs. The reputation as anti-hero is, in some ways, well earned by flouting traffic laws, but also through the presentation of self and lifestyle choices. Many messengers live a lifestyle well outside the mainstream. They are at once professionals who help to keep the wheels of capitalism turning, and they are individuals who resent "the system." Some talk of "ending the oil-igarchy" through a revolution that (paraphrasing Gil Scott-Heron) "will not be motorized." Sweat and grease come with the job, so appearance can be a low priority for many couriers (especially in the context of IC status), and couriers are jokingly said to exist solely on beer, bong-hits, and pizza. Though this is clearly an exaggeration, during a discussion about how to fuel the body for a long day's ride, a few couriers suggested peanut butter and jelly sandwiches, protein bars, tofu, or a big steak. One courier responded:

> Don't forget beer! Readily available carbohydrates, fiber, protein, calcium, potassium, phosphorus and vitamins B, B2, and B6. No cholesterol or fat. Plus it's cheap and portable, for when you don't have time for lunch.

While the numerous nutritional claims made on behalf of beer may be disputed, this messenger is certainly poking fun at the stereotypical beer-swilling cycle courier.

Such conceptions—celebrated by some messengers, abhorred by others—are used to damn the entire community by many in the media

and the larger society. National Public Radio's commentator Aaron
Freeman espoused this common view of messengers and their lunatic
antics:

> Reckless, testosterone-engorged bike messengers are agents not
> merely of business communication but Satan. They frighten our pe-
> destrians and annoy our drivers.

This commonplace stereotype is reflected in a 2004 UK poll com-
missioned by Horlicks (a brand of hot milk drinks, a subsidiary of
GlaxoSmithKline) found that bicycle couriers were number 3 on a UK
list of the least liked workers—below traffic wardens and bouncers,
above telephone sales representatives and politicians (Borkowski Press
Centre 2004).

What makes messengers unpopular—the perceived risk that they
pose to pedestrians—is required by the occupational structure. But the
character of that occupation has changed dramatically in the same years
that bike messengers have become more visible in the popular consciousness. The technological developments of the 1980s that enabled
increased productivity in the workplace displaced some of the need for
messengers. While the development of the personal computer did not
directly change the messenger industry, fax machines and email have
hurt the bread-and-butter of the occupation.

The introduction of fax machines and computers, along with the
revolution in information technology in the form of email and the Internet, has restructured the workplace in significant ways. This "second
industrial divide" (Piore and Sable 1984) has had multiple and contradictory consequences, depending on which analyst you believe. While some
argue that technology-based restructuring has resulted in increased democracy, autonomy, and a reduction in hierarchy in the workplace (Piore
and Sable 1984, Block 1990), others have argued that restructuring has
resulted in deskilling and a further proletarianization of the workforce
(Braverman 1974, Burawoy 1979, Shaiken 1984). Still others find no
clear pattern in the overall structures and reorganization of work, but try
instead to disaggregate the many sectors and professions to make sense
of the contradictory findings of others (Burris 1998, Liker et al 1999).
What is clear about the adoption of new technology in the contemporary
office is that many of the jobs that used to go to couriers are now done
with the click of a button on a computer or a speed-dial number on a fax.

But does this spell the end of the messenger industry? Newspapers
have reported a story about new technology replacing bike messengers
for many years. A steady stream of such articles has been published by

the New York *Times*, the Boston *Globe*, the Chicago *Tribune*, the San Francisco *Chronicle*, and the *Associated Press* between 1991 and 2007 (Baker 2005, Gutsche 2003, Hall 1992, McShane 1992, Mernin 1992, Staff 2007, Tomasson 1991). As far back as 1959, the famous author and New York *Times* journalist Gay Talese wrote an article about the demise of foot and bicycle messengers as Western Union modernized by adopting new technology (Talese 1959). To paraphrase Mark Twain, rumors of the death of bike messengers have been greatly exaggerated.

It is undeniable that fax machines and email have enabled documents to be transmitted across town in just a few moments, and this has significantly reduced the number of packages sent by courier. While there are some packages that will always need hard copies and signatures—especially in the judicial sector—many of the documents that messengers used to carry are now sent by fax or as email attachments. And so at the very moment in the 1990s when so many urban 19-year-olds wanted to become bike messengers, the need for messengers dropped drastically. The predictable outcome follows the normal laws of supply and demand: the combination of more messengers willing to do the job with less actual work to do has resulted in depressed wages and working conditions. As one messenger told the New York *Times*: "Now, more and more kids from the suburbs have found out that they can ride their bike and make $500 a week on their bicycle. And everyone comes rushing in, because who doesn't want to make $500 on their bicycle, and live in New York City?" (Weyland 2007). A messenger in a major city in the 1980s could expect to make several hundred dollars a week. At the start of the twenty-first century, this amount has not changed much, while inflation has greatly reduced the value of those few hundred dollars. The reduced buying power of the wages and the increased supply of willing workers have created a highly competitive work environment that presses messengers into taking greater risks to move materials faster. This further contributes to a reckless riding style, and thus to the low public opinion of messengers.

While the professional emphasis on skill and speed comes with a cultural emphasis on style, by far the vast majority of messengers are work-a-day folks who hang up their bike at the end of the shift after transporting take-out food or legal documents around the city. For example, the Cycle Messenger World Championships (CMWC) is an annual gathering of messengers to socialize, race, and build community. The 13th annual CMWC was held in New York City in July of 2005, and more than 1000 couriers showed up from across the globe. But of some 3000 messengers in the city, perhaps 10 percent rode across town for the weekend event. Almost as many non-messengers showed up from around the New York area to try their legs in racing against the "pros." Most messengers are not the urban anti-hero or lunatic on two wheels, but rather just folks trying to earn a meager wage. The dominant understanding of messengers as young white males riding fixed-gear bicycles who might otherwise be attending university or playing in a band is quite wrong. While the majority are typical low-wage service workers, the flashy stylistic cultural entrepreneurs, as seen in movies and on television commercials, are the ones who get the attention.

What enables a bike messenger to do the job so quickly is not just muscles and gears and creative (illegal) approaches to traffic; he also needs a radio or cell phone, a decidedly twenty-first century technology. How can nineteenth century technology co-exist with the latest wireless communications in a seamless version of fast capitalism? Processes of social change are clouded and crosscut with contingencies, and history is a process of both continuity and change (Lears 1981). In part due to the quirky traditional legal requirement of an original signature (and the fact that lawyers tend to push deadlines), and in part due to the geographic concentration of office space in the downtown core and the concomitant traffic, we see that sometimes the solution to the needs of fast capitalism is, in fact, a "slow" nineteenth-century technology: a guy on a bike can still get the package across town and into a client's hands faster and more cheaply than anything else.

Organizing the marginalized worker

There are many groups today that are truly indispensable to the smooth functioning of the economy and society in general. Imagine what our world would be like without people to take out the garbage, or without those who fix our toilet clogs. Garbage haulers and plumbers are relatively well paid for their work; partially in recognition that few people would like to replace them. These are also traditionally white male working-class jobs, which also means higher wages than jobs that traditionally belong to more marginal groups.

Other workers are similarly essential to society yet still suffer from low wages. Without migrant laborers in the agricultural fields, our food prices would skyrocket. Without janitors pushing their late night brooms our schools, offices, and public spaces would be inhospitable (or we would have to clean up after ourselves). Low-cost landscapers tend the homes of the upper class, their young are minded by nannies, and their rooms tidied by housecleaners. But these jobs are rarely unionized, are generally poorly remunerated, and often come with little job security. And of course the racial component of these sectors is undeniable: lower-paid professions are more likely to be dominated by non-whites. The working conditions are also likely dirtier and less safe.

Workers subjected to these conditions develop predicable responses. Many retreat to a passive position of acceptance and "go along to get along." Others agitate for change, sometimes winning union recognition as Cesar Chavez and Dolores Huerta did with the United Farm Workers (UFW). But the challenges to organizing marginal workers are myriad. Some workers do not speak up because they fear losing their jobs. Others believe that fighting the owners is not possible (the UFW slogan *Si se puede! –* "Yes we can!" explicitly argued against this). Still other workers come to believe not only that changing the system is not possible, but that it is not worthwhile. This obstacle is cultural: workers buy in to the system and help to reproduce hegemony. When workers unquestioningly accept an individualist orientation, when they agree to the dictates of the market, when they abide by the rules of the system, they accede to the worldview of those with power over them. The mainstream labor unions in the US do not challenge these assumptions, and thus they contribute to the reproduction of capitalism. Many marginal and mainstream workers embrace individualism and the pursuit of the American Dream, hoping that they will be the next ones to make it big. This competition amongst the working class for the few available resources keeps them from uniting and addressing broader interests. It is thus functional for the capitalist system as a whole.

Unlike many groups forced to compete for scarce resources at the economic margins, messengers have not succumbed to individualism, cut-throat competition, or collaboration. Though their work is often done alone in traffic and their economic and spatial marginalization contributes to competitive individualistic orientations, couriers also organize together to address the negative aspects of the industry. They know that they are indispensable to the smooth functioning of business in their cities, as one Washington DC messenger said:

> Whether it's San Fran, DC, London, New York . . . Without us there would be no function in any city . . . We make lawyers make money. Everyone makes money off of us. And if we were to stop in one city there would be no more business.

Couriers with this consciousness have formed Bicycle Messenger Associations (BMAs) in most major US cities, along with national BMAs and an International Bicycle Messenger Association. Canadian couriers now belong to the same labor union as postal employees (CUPE). Several US cities have also successfully established labor unions, and affiliation drives are underway in several more locations (Curtis 1998, Hoover 1999, King and Van Praet 2004). Like labor unions, BMAs address the typical labor concerns of hours, wages, and working conditions. The BMAs and unions have also taken on the media's often-inaccurate portrayal of messengers by writing letters to the editor of local papers, and have engaged in politics on behalf of messengers by similarly writing to administrators to complain about unsafe conditions. One example followed the death of Sebastian Lukomski in London on 23 February 2004. Seb was the seventh documented messenger to be run over by a Heavy Goods Vehicle (HGV), a type of truck that weighs more than 7.5 metric tons. Bill Chidley, the Chair of the London BMA, wrote to the Mayor of London and the various political parties with representation in the city. While the city officials and party representatives have taken the LBMA seriously, little actual change has taken place.

Independent contractor status is a particularly important target for many messengers, and some success with altering official policy has been achieved in a few states. BMAs and individual messengers have continually challenged independent contractor status, battle by battle. One recent case involved a messenger who chafed at being an IC and yet forced to wear a company shirt, a clear case of being an employee and not being an employee at the same time. Another messenger offered a solution:

> You are a very visible entity in your town, simply by doing what you do for a living. More people will have close contact with you than with any other ad media. I'm not advocating messengers as riding billboards, but you do have access to a captive audience like no other ad medium. How about suggesting compensation for the use of your prime ad space. This way they can get the shirt on you, and you will benefit from extra income. Selling out? Depends on how you look at it. We don't make the most stellar wage for the dangerous job we do, and more dough is always good. OR . . . you can tell them you are an INDEPENDANT CONTRACTOR and the only logo you are obliged to wear is that of your own company.

Another messenger replied:

> Or you and your associates could wear the shirts while plotting the
> downfall of this IC bullshit. If the company is going to force you to
> do things, you can force it to deal with you as a human being with la-
> bor rights. Then you could get workers comp, unemployment, and
> maybe more money if you fight for it.

Lack of health care is a particularly important issue for many messengers (primarily in the US, as Canadian and many European messengers have a nationalized health care system to rely on). Due to IC status, any accident that happens "on the job" may have few necessary repercussions for the delivery company in terms of worker's compensation claims. Many messengers avoid any such claims (whether due to ignorance or IC status), and instead get health care where they can (which usually means either a county hospital or none at all). One innovative solution to this is the Bicycle Messenger Emergency Fund (BMEF), a non-profit that was started by an enterprising and civic-minded former messenger (discussed further in Chapter 4).

Conclusion

The job of the messenger, then, is to convey packages across town as quickly and cheaply as possible. Messengers work within a necessary, though marginalized, occupation, and do so for low wages under risky conditions. They are subject to all the exploitation and alienation that Marx identified 150 years ago, but in some ways technological change has made their job both easier and more difficult. As with many sectors under fast capitalism, new technology means greater efficiency, but it has also meant lower wages. The piece-rate system means that messengers must increase their risky behaviors to beat time and compress the space of the city, and this leads to reckless riding—or the perception of recklessness by the public. Though they are an easily identifiable part of the urban core, in some ways to survive and make a living wage messengers must strive to remain invisible. But by weaving in and out of traffic, occupying a marginal space where they are both seen and not seen and thus relieving themselves of traffic's burden, messengers can maximize their low pay. By co-operating within the system, messengers help to reproduce these very circumstances of their employment, and support the broader system of capitalism by delivering packages quickly and cheaply. The dark shadow cast by these creative approaches to traffic is the daily fact of risk. Riding quickly through the city is a dangerous proposition. The next chapter explores the sociology of voluntary risk-taking behavior.

Notes

1 A messenger quoted in Caroline H. Dworin's article "Wings on their heels." *The New York Times* 14 November 2008.

2. This poses a challenge for messengers in the post-9/11 moment. Messengers already suffer disproportionate disrespect and prejudicial treatment when compared to their fellow delivery service workers who drive trucks and wear uniforms. Most packages delivered by messengers carry minimal inscriptions and often no address or identifying markers. Add to this that messengers generally do not wear uniforms, often appear unkempt and dirty, and carry an assortment of odd bike tools in their bags, and the result is that many messengers have struggled to make timely deliveries due to being held up by building security. I had countless experiences during the anthrax scare of early 2002 when it took a precious 15 minutes to get through security into office buildings and the State Capitol to make deliveries.

3. Of course "welfare" is not limited to out-of-work individuals or seniors. The economic crisis of 2008-09 has seen massive corporate welfare payouts to foundering banks, insurance companies, and auto manufacturers.

4. A snakebite is called this because the tube is pinched against the metal wheel rim, causing two small symmetrical punctures, as if bitten by the teeth of a snake.

3. Risk, Edgework, and the Community of Danger

"You gotta be aggressive in the city, or else, you know, something's gonna happen. You gotta be like a car, you gotta act like a car. Think of it sort of like a chess game."[1]

The structure of the messenger industry drives couriers to ride aggressively in a full-speed, three-dimensional, high-stakes chess game against a powerful opponent who is probably paying no attention to you. Messengers have to plot out the likely moves of drivers who are not thinking about cyclists at all, they must do so at the speed of traffic, while physically exerting themselves, and any mistake could be fatal. For the courier on the job, space and time become elastic, and the reality of risk is ever-present.

Marginality and CitySpace

Messengers have to metaphorically compress space and time and get their packages across town as quickly as possible. The distance between the pick up point and the delivery address can be thought of in terms of miles, or blocks, or minutes. Though couriers operate moving vehicles, they are not quite cars and certainly aren't pedestrians. They are somewhere in between these two categories, physically marginalized to the sides of the street, but not allowed on the sidewalks.

The bicycle messenger is, thus, simultaneously a temporal and spatial subject that exists in a network of power. Urban planners design the streets, laws govern the flow of traffic, and the needs of commerce dictate, in a utilitarian way, how the spaces of the city are built through accretion over time. The courier does not get to define her space, but she can improvise to create an effective area. She cannot compete with the power of a car, but she can easily outmaneuver one. The space of a city, the flow of traffic, and therefore the reality of a messenger's day is affected by political, economic, cultural, and historical factors. These several structural forces combine through contingent and sequential circumstances to define the landscape of the city. What I call CitySpace, what the bicycle messenger navigates daily, has been built layer-by-layer in space, and moment-by-moment over time. To understand the courier's workplace, we must look at how the space of the city has changed sequentially and contingently through history (Burawoy 1992: 281, Gilbert and Wehr 2003).

A spatially and historically sensitive sociology looks to the past to understand how society changes over time. Social processes exist in particular places and times, and this context is important to understanding their meanings. The contingent moment of a process matters, but so too does the sequence of events. Our modern, jumbled QWERTY keyboard looks the way it does because early typewriters could not keep up with the first typists—the keys had to be mixed up to slow them down. Similarly, modern industrial milk production originated during the massive urban growth of 1930s Los Angeles, where rising land prices, strong demand, and the cultural knowledge of Portuguese immigrants enabled industrial-style confinement dairying. The contingent moment, the sequence of events, cultural peculiarities, and the specific place matters greatly to how society changes (Abbott 1991, Calhoun 1998, Gilbert and Wehr 2003, Liebowitz and Margolis 1995, Smith 1991, Tilly 1981, Tilly 1984).

The modern period, David Harvey (1989) argues, has annihilated space by compressing time. We cannot truly separate space and time, and so we must analyze them as a continuum of sequence and contingency, and must do so while keeping in mind the context of social power. The control of space is an important form of power, and this "articulates with control over time, as well as with money and other forms of social power" in an important nexus (Harvey 1989: 226). Capitalists, for instance, have a great interest in controlling the space of the factory. By compressing space and time they can increase turnover rates. Frederick W. Taylor invented the concept of scientific management in 1895. Taylorism, or Fordism as it came to be known when Henry Ford applied the process to great effect on his auto assembly line, was a process of labor control through the piece-rate system, which gave an incentive to workers to be more efficient. Taylorism ostensibly brought the interests of the worker into line with those of management; with the piece-rate system, both groups had a financial stake in speed, perfection, and increased output. Under Taylorism, the foreman of a factory does not allow any wasted movement by workers on an assembly line. The smallest of gestures is recorded, analyzed for efficiency, and the worker is disciplined to ensure maximum productivity. Time and space are organized on the factory floor to maximize profit and control (Foucault 1979, Haber 1964).

The state has its own interests in the control of people and space. Though we take the state's continued viability for granted today, in the early days of the modern nation-state several things were required to ensure its continued existence. The state needed taxes to fund its actions, it needed conscripts to populate the military, and it needed well-defined borders. The modern nation-state has an interest in controlling a distinct space and categorizing the inhabitants of that area for purposes of taxation and conscription (Scott 1998). These state interests are interlocked with the interests of capital. The state and capital both require continued economic growth. Without an expanding economy capital cannot realize profit and the state will experience a decline in tax revenue. This produces a budget shortfall and a fiscal crisis that threatens the state's continued legitimacy (Evans 1995; O'Connor 1973). Jimmy Carter's loss to Ronald Reagan in 1980 is in part attributable to such processes, as is the 2003 recall of California's Governor Gray Davis following the "dot.com bust." As well as agreement on the need for an expanding economy, there is an affinity between capitalists and state officials for the construction of space-annihilating structures such as roads, airports, and other infrastructure (Wehr 2004).

Such space-annihilating structures help meet the needs of modern daily life. The landscape of the city—roads, buildings, sidewalks, driveways, and parking areas—have been constructed for maximum ease-of-use by the automobile driver, with the interests of pedestrians a close second (pedestrians are often understood by urban planners as car drivers who have just parked). The city and its transportation networks are primarily organized around the production and consumption of commodities—the smooth flow of traffic is crucial for both industry and retail businesses. David Macauley has identified the sidewalk as an increasingly marginalized space due to the ascendancy of automobile travel. Sidewalks, he argues, are "in one sense the exteriors and margins of the roads" and "in another sense they are now the thresholds of storefronts, houses and parks that they ring." (2000: 36). From the nineteenth century to the present moment, walking has moved from being the central transportation activity in the city to being what people do between their cars and their final destinations. Sidewalks have become less important than roads, but are they still important to business.

Cities were originally designed, of course, for pedestrians, travelers on horseback, and horse-drawn carriages. With the invention of the bicycle, ironically enough, cyclists formed associations to lobby for the paving of roads. Bicycles in larger cities would get hopelessly mired in the mud, manure, and muck of the late-nineteenth century city, and pavement was seen as the solution. A cyclist advocacy group with 100,000 members, the League of American Wheelmen (founded in 1880), lobbied for and won the partial paving of many cities, just before the assembly line made feasible the mass production of autos (Culley 2001: 257).

With the increase in availability and affordability of the automobile, Americans became much more mobile. But cars were not a central part of everyday American life until the post-World War II rise of the American middle class and its eventual race-based flight to the suburbs. This rise of the middle class occurred in tandem with several changes in the structure of industry and society. Shifts in occupational structure (primarily the inclusion of women into jobs they were previously excluded from), shifts in industry and labor processes (the expanded importance of defense, technology, and the de-skilling of labor), and alliances between previously isolated elite groups (Eisenhower's famous military industrial complex) provided the opportunity for the formation of an American middle class with its own social identity (Baxandall and Gordon 1995; Braverman 1974; Burawoy 1982; Lotchin 1992; Mills 1951; Mills 1956).

From the late-nineteenth century and into the late-twentieth century, then, sidewalks moved from marginal to vital and back to marginal, with the area between the road and the sidewalk becoming a new marginal space. It is this area that is inhabited by cyclists. Messengers in particular have found this marginal space between traffic, parked cars, and pedestrians to be a market niche. They operate at the margins of the systems of power that construct space and time within the city, and their improvisations mean that they can travel quickly and easily (Boyle 2004). This produces the service-commodity of speedy package delivery within the confines of a city designed for other groups, classes, and vehicles. But the use of this margin is fraught with risk: cars may cross this space to turn or park, pedestrians may step out from between parked cars, and drivers may open car doors into an on-coming rider. Bicycle messengers must pay attention to all of these likelihoods as they go about delivering packages.

The banality of risk

So why do they do it? Why do these individuals throw themselves into traffic with minimal protections—many without even a helmet? How could anyone ride into the streets day after day dueling with cars, taxis, and buses that outweigh them by thousands of pounds and have massive acceleration and torque advantages? The answer is both social-psychological and structural: there are socially defined individual-level notions of risk, group-level dynamics of culture, and political-economic structures of opportunity. But at base, to paraphrase Hannah Arrendt, it is the banality of risk.

The popular notion about those who take risks in their occupations or their leisure time is that they must be "thrill seekers" or "adrenaline junkies" who search for extreme forms of excitement and entertainment in order to fulfill some deep-seated psychological desire or biological need. While there may be some level of predisposition towards risk-taking behavior such as bicycle messengering, such theories as "thrill-seekers versus the risk-averse" do not tell us about the social context of risk and the role of community and cultural support. Messengering is a fully social endeavor, and as such we must view the interplay of structure and agency in understanding why messengers do what they do, and take the risks they take. People make history, Marx said, but not under conditions of their own choosing. Individuals make choices and exercise their free will, but they do so within certain structural constraints. Following Pierre Bourdieu's (1977) notion of "structural improvisation," we must understand the "free choice" of taking a messenger job within the structural conditions imposed by the capitalist market, state regulation of the economy and society, and cultural sanctions and opportunities.

Risk is a collective endeavor, not simply the free choice of an individual. Everyone engages in risky behavior on a daily basis: walking across the street, eating in a restaurant, smoking, drinking, and having sex all entail a certain amount of risk. But the idea of what qualifies as risky behavior is socially constructed. Having unsafe sex with a stranger under the influence of controlled substances probably counts as "risky" to many, and yet people engage in this behavior recreationally. Getting into a car is more risky than riding in an airplane, and yet most people are more comfortable with driving than with flying. Though a rational individual might assess the records of the many airlines and fly only with the safest (like Dustin Hoffman's character in the film "Rainman"), most people, most of the time, make the mundane choice based on price or what airline they have a frequent-flyer card with. Like beauty, risk is in the eye of the beholder (Douglas 1992, Hari 2005, Sivak et al 1991).

On the abstract structural level, many sociologists have suggested that risk has increased in modern times. Ulrich Beck (1992) argues that the emergence of risk in everyday life is a hallmark of the contemporary moment. The rise of a "new modernity" characterized as reflexive modernization (Beck notably does not use the term post-modern) is rooted in technological advances that have brought new levels of risk. With industrialization came risk, but it was not recognized publicly, nor was it regulated in any meaningful way by either capital or the state. As society moves towards a new stage, this risk is recognized and attempts at mitigation are made. [2] Global climate change is an example of this process: Industrial capitalism since the 1800s has loaded the atmosphere with unsustainable levels of carbon dioxide and "greenhouse gasses" which have severely altered the climate. 200 years later we are experiencing global climate change with perhaps irreversible results. This level of risk was not known when coal was first burned, nor was it predicted when the internal combustion engine was first attached to four wheels and mass produced for the public. Over the last 30 years, the risks to health, human life, and the global environment have become clear, but only very recently has society proposed steps toward solutions.[3]

But risk is not something that floats freely—it is concretely undertaken by specific people and groups for particular reasons. Stephen Lyng (1990) examines voluntary risk-taking among small groups and individuals where there is a fine line between safety and danger. "Edgework" is an activity in which "an individual's failure to meet the challenge at hand will result in death or, at the very least, debilitating injury" (1990: 857).

People engaged in edgework voluntarily undertake risky activities, in Lyng's analysis, out of a social-psychological response to structural conditions: under the alienation-inducing conditions of capitalism, people must seek fulfillment in realms other than work (Lasch 1978). While most people are pushed towards fulfillment via commodity consumption in the market, others are pushed towards edgework to shock them out of the dullness of the daily grind—they attempt to find authenticity in risky activities (Holyfield and Jonas 2003). Risky leisure time activities offer a level of fulfillment that work cannot. Yet messengers seem to have it both ways: they get to work and play at the same time—their work, while alienating, also offers them the instant fulfillment of the playful, yet risky endeavor.

The specialized skill involved in such risky ventures as skydiving, car racing, or rock climbing gives the practitioner not only a demonstrable claim of ability, but a feeling of exhilaration and the transcendence of routine normalcy. The risky activities often necessitate a high level of attention and concentration, described by some as "mental toughness." Practitioners of edgework may translate this ability to other areas, giving them and their fellows a sense of elitism over those who have not faced and overcome such risks and obstacles.

Lyng gives occupational examples such as combat and police work, both areas that involve a great deal of risk in everyday work settings. Notably, like soldiers and police officers, messengers often refer to those who do not face such risk in their lives as "citizens," in order to differentiate themselves as an elite. One Vietnam veteran described messengering as coming as close to "the shit" as he had ever seen in a normal, state-side job.

Messengering is a form of edgework: it entails voluntary risk-taking that puts the participant at risk of death or bodily injury. But messengering poses several problems regarding this concept. Lyng suggests that edgework is "a type of experiential anarchy in which the individual moves beyond the realm of established social patterns to the very fringes of ordered reality" (1990: 882). While many use the term anarchy as a popular synonym for "chaos," it is more accurately understood as a political theory of self-organization (Bakunin 1971; Kropotkin 2002, Proudhon 2003 [1851]). Jeff Ferrell elaborates on the ways that the political stance of anarchism is an exemplary form of edgework (Ferrell 2005: 75). But is chaos what lays on the other side of the edge? For messengers, edgework does not move a participant towards chaos so much as it changes the rules of behavior that apply. Risky activity increases the amount of stochastic intrusion into the order of daily life, yet as Lyng points out (1990: 874), there are ritualistic aspects to skydiving that put a premium on predictability and order in the face of the potential for disorder to appear during a jump—jumpers spend much more time preparing for the jump than they do actually falling.

Similarly, on city streets, messengers do not face chaos so much as an ordered reality that conforms to different rules than most job sites. There are subtle rules to the behavior of drivers in traffic that must be learned by the "rookie" messenger. Most drivers understand that traffic laws are more like suggestions unless there is a police officer present, hence traffic can be unpredictable at first glance. Yet a messenger who has worked the streets long enough learns to look at traffic and see the potential hazards: they learn what the real rules are. As one veteran New York City messenger put it, "Messengers have better instincts and re-flexes, and a lot sharper peripheral vision. . . . If you're not conscious and in the moment at all times, you can die on someone's car door. That's what separates us" from other riders (Staff 2005).

Do messengers have sharper reflexes or instincts? I think it's true, but not as an inherent trait; it is something one learns. I realized that I had "gotten it," ironically enough, when I had a crash after a long day at work. I was off the clock, having ridden perhaps 50 miles that day. I was grimy, tired, riding home in heavy commuter traffic, and it was starting to get dark. As I was going down a hill, reaching perhaps 20 mph, I reached under my seat to turn on a blinking safety light so that cars would be more likely to see me. When I looked up I saw that I was in the midst of street construction. The workers had quit for the day, but they laid a huge steel plate over their excavation pit, with asphalt mounded up around to keep it in place. I hit the mound and my bike and I went into the air. I brought my other hand up from the light and grabbed the han-dlebars. Time slowed down. I flew through the air for perhaps ten feet, landing with a wobble and immediately began a skid to slow down. I seemed to register time flicking by in microseconds. I saw that I was going to ride directly into a parked car, but if I steered back into the bike lane I would likely lose control and fall into oncoming traffic. So I could hit the back of the car, ruining my wheel and likely injuring myself badly. Or I could steer to the other side of the parked car. Somehow as I covered those 10 feet, slowing from 20 to maybe 15 mph, I noticed that the car I was about to hit was parked fairly far out from the curb. I steered in between the auto and the curb . . . thinking "I might just make this!" until my handlebar caught the wing mirror of the car and I was thrown to the ground on the grass between the curb and the sidewalk, suffering nothing more than grass stains on my pants. Luck? Perhaps. But also a degree of good instincts, quick reflexes, the ability to maintain presence of mind and pay attention to every detail, and knowing precisely what I could do under the circumstances. I'm still amazed that I didn't kill myself.

So messengers develop instincts and reflexes that help keep them alive. This elitist stance might ring false to many commuters, but at least a few will recognize the learning process that anyone goes through with enough city riding. I went through a typical process when I became a courier. After commuting by bike to school and work, I thought I knew a thing or two. I had become alert to how to look for the driver's silhouette in parked cars to anticipate a car door opening into bike-space. I learned how to pay attention to the cars ahead and give myself enough room to allow for surprise lane changes or impromptu turns. But the move from commuter to messenger changes this dynamic both quantitatively and qualitatively. As a commuter I was on the road for 20 or 30 minutes at a time, as a messenger I was riding with a purpose all day. What were once basic guidelines about drivers' behavior (look for the parking car, allow plenty of room) morphed into the perception of subtle cues that came to be second nature. I began to see how cars would move slightly to the right or left in the lane, and I learned that this slight drift, even when there was no turn signal, indicated that the driver was going to turn. I stopped just watching for pedestrians waiting to dodge out between parked cars and began to notice those that were hailing taxis. Cabs will dart across several lanes of traffic to pick up a fare, regardless of the lowly courier in their path.

All cyclists must attend to these urban facts, as they can become matters of life and death. But messengers pick up these cues much more quickly since they are on the streets for hours at a stretch. One messenger jokingly called this anticipation process "extending my antennae" to sense what drivers would do up ahead; she suggested that when tuned to "high" her antennae could detect things blocks ahead and around the corner. As Lynn Breedlove (2002: 3) put it in her account of messenger-ing in San Francisco:

> You take everything in, you don't miss nothing, the whole street and
> things coming at you from around corners as you round corners, and
> you can see things before they appear to the non-messenger eye, you
> can see through buildings, you can look down a cross street before

> you even get to it, half prophesy, half feel, half hear the way's clear.
> You have to if you want to survive and deliver the package on time.

This anticipation, the subtle reading of the rules of the road, can feel to the messenger as if she knows what a driver will do before the driver even knows it—similar to Lyng's identification of edgework cultivating an "elite" or even "immortal" perspective. But this reading of cues is a structured activity, predictable and orderly and far from chaotic. It is, however, self-organized. The rules are not written anywhere—they are informal and unofficial. And yet they come about through interaction and on some level mutual agreement—knowing them comes from experience and skill and a good bit of dumb luck at living long enough to understand the patterns. For instance, a minivan is predictably unpredictable: a soccer mom dialing a cell phone, swilling a cappuccino, and soothing the baby might erratically change lanes at any moment and the seasoned messenger will give her a wide berth. A police officer, on the other hand, is unpredictably unpredictable: 99 percent of the time they scrupulously follow the rules of the road. But without warning—and sometimes without lights and sirens at first—cops might dodge across three lanes of traffic to turn in a split second.

The negotiation of risk is a learned behavior, though the lessons vary from messenger to messenger. As one veteran put it in a newspaper interview, rookies get injured more often because they are too cautious: "You're usually not aggressive until you know what you're doing, so the ones who are not aggressive are the ones who get into accidents" (Mohammed 2002). Another messenger told the New York *Times*: "You gotta be aggressive in the city, or else, you know, something's gonna happen. You gotta be like a car, you gotta act like a car. Think of it sort of like a chess game" (Weyland 2007). And yet another veteran said that he was too aggressive when he first started, and now is much more careful: "I consider myself a very safe rider and I don't take any chances, or the chances I do take are well planned. . . . When you have a three or five minute deadline, you do it right" (Staff 2003). Riders negotiate the risk of edgework through aggression,[4] but also by learning the ropes and taking planned chances.

William Cockerham (2006: 13) offers a more social approach to risk-taking behavior by considering variables like gender, class, and race. Lupton (1999) has argued that risk is a gendered behavior, with males much more likely to undertake risky behavior than females, and young males even more so. This is evident in crime statistics (Steffensmeier and Allan 1995), and Harris et al (2002) have persuasively shown that an attitude of having "nothing to lose" pushes risk-taking behaviors. This, of course, is highly influenced by social structural forces; some populations are more likely to have "nothing to lose" than others. The interplay of structural constraints and agenic choices can yield a highly race-, class-, gender-, and age-inflected likelihood of risk taking—a reality that we see played out in the diverse community of bicycle messengers. Cockerham (2006: xv-xvi) argues that risk is a social endeavor in every sense: its origins are in social groups and actions are often undertaken for a particular audience, who provide support or encouragement. He posits a continuum of risk-taking behavior:

> At the high end are risk-takers like participants in extreme sports who actively seek out risks and have the resources to engage in these daring activities. . . . Other risk-takers, in contrast, are at the lower end of the risk-response continuum. These are passive risk-takers who take risks because the structure of their social life leaves them with little or no choice.

This is supported by the work of Harris et al (2002) who show that the attitude of having "nothing to lose" can influence delinquent or risky behavior among adolescents. High-level risk takers, on the other hand, do so because it makes them feel good (Cockerham 2006: 124), not only in terms of adrenaline or the thrill, but also in terms of the social approval of a real or potential audience. Risk-taking behavior can offer them a sense of elitism or authenticity as compared with the daily grind of the workplace. For those on the low end of Cockerham's continuum, risk *is* the daily grind of the workplace. So there is a symbolic level of the interaction involved in the broad context of risk taking: the meaning of the risk—the perception of the situation—is socially constructed by and for both the risk-taker and the audience.

At the high end of the risk continuum are the extreme athletes, and there is a clear overlap between the demographics of some messengers and participants in extreme sports like snowboarding, skateboarding, skydiving, or bungee jumping: young, white, and male. Messengering is similar, but with important differences, as many messengers are non-white, poor or working class, and structurally disadvantaged. Most messengers simply work on their bikes as a way to make a meager living, not because it's cool, fashionable, or risky. So messengers are at both ends of Cockerham's continuum. Many people do it because they have little other choice of gainful employment. Others choose it because it's cool and edgy. But sometimes a single individual may represent both ends of the continuum; in some cases people who are just trying to make a living evolve to embody the social behavior of actively seeking the thrill and joining those in the high-end of the continuum.

The members of Team Puma are illustrative here. Team Puma is a group of New York City messengers, led by veteran messenger Kevin "Squid" Bolger. Inspired by Olympic medal-winning former NYC messenger Nelson Vails, Squid put together the team to compete in professional races, and secured sponsorship from Puma, the athletic clothing manufacturer. Many of these messengers fit the young white male category, and many ride flashy bikes with a great deal of style. But they also are work-a-day messengers trying to feed their families; getting a free bike and some athletic gear sponsored by the Puma Company would seem like a good deal for a working-class kid from Brooklyn. These racers, then, occupy an in-between space in the continuum of risk, both actively seeking out risk like those at the high end, but doing so in part because of the social and economic structure that they find themselves in, as with those at the low end of the risk spectrum.

As is demonstrated by the sponsorship of Team Puma, risk has become commodified, as seen most clearly with packaged trips to the top of Mount Everest (Palmer 2002). Yet with such adventures there is a counter-intuitive erasure of danger in some extreme sports. Palmer argues that in such "tourist-oriented versions of extreme sports, the very real prospect of injury and death has been stripped from the activity itself," and this is due in no small part to the commodification of risk as a selling point for extreme vacations (Palmer 2002). What Team Puma does is navigate a line between danger and sport. The team is drawn from the ranks of messengers who have sharpened their skills on the street under risky conditions. But they compete on a closed, safe track in the controlled environment of the velodrome against seasoned athletes. Such risk, then, becomes a selling point for athletic clothing, while ironically being stripped away from the actual competitive event.

While there is not yet a tourist package of messengering vacations, there are many "citizens" or "tourists" who have taken up the style of messengers, from the clothes and bag to the bicycle and the attitude (discussed more deeply in Chapter 4). These individuals, known in the messenger world as "posengers" (a cross between the words poseur and messenger) or "fakengers" now show up at messenger events regularly. This has caused a certain amount of consternation, with some couriers wanting to keep posengers out of the community. Others argue in favor of allowing posengers into races in order to take their money, because in most unofficial messenger events all riders will contribute an entry fee, which is pooled and split among the top finishers. In these cases, more riders, especially inexperienced riders, simply means more money for the winners—who are usually the messengers.

What is not under question is the result of having inexperienced riders on the racecourse: more crashes and more injuries. I saw on accident happen at the 2005 CMWC in New York City at a particularly dangerous point on the racecourse where riders could go straight or make a U-turn—those taking a turn would need to swing out to the right and then cut across the whole lane to make the turn while riders going straight would keep left to avoid the slower, turning riders. This clearly makes for a dangerous situation with slow riders crossing the lane as faster riders blew by. The solution was to simply signal that you were making a turn, and the rider behind would adjust accordingly. In the accident I saw, a rider made a turn without signaling and took out three veteran NYC messengers, sending one to the hospital. I later talked to the rider who caused the accident—he was a student from a local university, a "posenger" who wanted to race because it was a cool thing to do. His search for coolness and authenticity put three riders off of their jobs for a significant time. So while messengering does not sell risk as the Everest outfitters do, it does offer a possibility to outsiders in search of a community of risk and danger. This young man capitalized on the symbolic risk of participating in a messenger race in a fairly simple manner: he just signed up and rode his bike with the rest of the racers. This is not traditional commodification, as with risky vacation packages sold to those suffering from middle-class ennui. But there is a denial of the real level of risk on the part of the inexperienced rider, and a concomitant increase in risk to veteran riders. Risk, in short, comes to be seen as a relatively banal part of a messenger's day, and the blasé attitude ironically enables the symbolic appropriation of this risk by fakengers.

Risk-taking behavior, then, can be seen as both an economic necessity for some, and yet also a dangerous and emotionally charged adventure into authenticity. Jennifer Lois (2003) has explored the intersection of voluntary risk and emotions in the case of search and rescue volunteers. She found layers of emotional responses to the heroic efforts of mountain rescuers as they labored to save the lives of lost tourists. "Emotional cool" is the ability to manage or suppress one's emotions during critical moments of a rescue. Though few see messengers as heroes, couriers must deal with similar layers of emotion in their work: from anger to aggression to elation.

Where does this urge for authenticity come from? In his 2005 elaboration on the theoretical foundations of edgework, Lyng variously connects to several theories. He argues that the desire for feelings of authenticity is akin to Weber's notion of the re-enchantment of the world, a response to over-determination and the iron cage of rationality. Then Lyng follows Baudrillard in identifying a yearning for authenticity within the confines of hyper-reality. Finally, building upon the ideas of Foucault, Lyng suggests that edgework can be seen as a transgression of societally-imposed boundaries (Lyng 2005: 24, 26, 35, 45-47). But this can also be seen through the more basic lens of political economy. As discussed earlier, social-economic structures alienate workers and leave us feeling unfulfilled in our work lives. Various hobbies may offer release. Scholars from a Critical Theory perspective argue that we consume mass-produced commodities that are marketed as offering fulfillment (Horkheimer and Adorno 1944), with contemporary examples being a vacation trip up Mount Everest or a bungee-jumping outing. But on the low end of the risk-continuum, voluntary risk-taking can offer access to a heightened emotional state that practitioners consider "more real," "more cool," or more authentic than other forms of employment. Indeed, though this semi-skilled labor is not well-paid, messengers can cash in on their cultural capital, as the Team Puma riders have. This process is thus political-economic and cultural as well as emotional.

As couriers navigate the dangers of the street in the daily grind of delivering parcels, they must maintain their emotional cool in the press of traffic, in the face of road rage, and in order to fulfill the imperative of speedy deliveries. This form of voluntary risk-taking is, in short, a rather banal affair. Messengers learn the tricks of the trade, the subtle cues of traffic, and the methods of becoming invisible in the inner-city. For the majority of messengers, risk is just part of the job. And yet for some it is also what attracts them to the occupation, enabling them to escape the confines of alienation, normalcy, and the day-to-day tedium of the modern world.

The Daily Grind: Dueling with cars, cabs, and buses

In cities developed for cars, there is an understandable sense of ownership that a driver feels when negotiating the roadways. When a driver comes upon a cyclist there is always potential for an altercation—and just as much potential for co-operation. Many drivers feel that cyclists should always stick to the right-hand side of the road—and indeed this is essentially the law in many states. Messengers, on the other hand, know that they can weave in and out of traffic without impeding the overall flow of the cars in the road—and that they have to in order to get packages delivered on time. Car commuters more than professional cab- or bus-drivers seem to be especially incensed at the sight of cyclists floating by them, and the incidence of road rage by drivers towards cyclists is unfortunately common.

Many couriers subscribe to the idea of "exposure time," the straightforward principle (adopted from warfare) that the more you ride, the more you are exposed to the perils that come with the job. Messengers score high on the exposure meter, while bike commuters score low. With increased exposure time comes an increased likelihood of accidents. An average cyclist can expect to have a major accident once every 2000 miles (Culley 2001: 127). Commuters may ride 2000 miles in a year while serious bicycle racers may ride three times this number of miles in a season of training—though they are typically not riding in heavy traffic. Messengers, on the other hand, often log this number of miles in heavy traffic in two months of working the streets. Yet messengers do not suffer more than the average number of cycling accidents in a year. The difference is skill: Messengers often have the ability to avoid harm in traffic due to knowledge and experience. Most messengers do not suffer a serious accident once a month because the same increase in exposure means an increase in knowledge about the rhythms of traffic. My own experience is emblematic. I've had two serious accidents in more than 20 years of riding in the streets, one ending in a hospital visit (luckily I only had bruises). Both happened before I was a messenger. The numerous close-calls that I had as a courier all came from the carelessness of drivers juggling a cell phone and a coffee cup during a heavy commute time. Only twice did I go down in traffic as a courier, and neither case involved a driver being at fault—first was the incident described above after work, and second when I turned too sharply on a street packed with two inches of snow. It was a stupid, amateurish mistake, and I was lucky that there were no cars around. But in the main, messengers learn the rules of the road, gather knowledge that accrues with exposure time, and develop a skill set that means more near misses, but fewer actual accidents. Messengers quite simply learn the skills and cultivate the foresight to avoid many common traffic problems.

What is counter-intuitive is the stance that many messengers take regarding helmets. It would seem obvious that those who are exposed to great risk would take basic precautions like wearing a helmet, bright clothes, or reflective materials. Yet many of these protections do not conform to the cultural expressions of cool, or masculine postures of toughness. There is also geographic variation. Riders in some cites all wear helmets, such as the one that I worked in. In fact, helmet use was required by the owner of the company I worked for, but most riders wore them regardless of the company rules. In New York City, on the other hand, the style is to go without. Some companies require their riders to wear protective headgear, others either don't care, or can't insist because they hire riders as independent contractors.

A study of Boston bike messengers found that the rate of bicycle courier workplace injury and lost time far exceeded that of other risky industries. The national average number of general workdays lost per year is 3.0 per 100 workers. In risky occupations, such as meatpacking, the average is 11.0 days lost per 100 workers. Dennerlein and Meeker (2002) showed that Boston messengers lost 47 workdays per 100 work- ers, a result the authors call "staggering." The study (the only one ever done on messengers, and one that the authors themselves consider "pre- liminary") showed that 77 percent of Boston couriers viewed their job as involving a fair to serious amount of risk, and 90 percent of them had been injured on the job, with 70 percent missing at least one day of work from the injury. A reasonable person might assume that those who carry the most risk would compensate for that risk by adopting safety meas- ures, and scholarly studies of recreational cyclists have found this to be true (Rodgers 1996). Yet in the Boston study only 24 percent of couriers wore a helmet "most of the time" or "all of the time" (Dennerlein and Meeker 2002). Why would someone voluntarily increase their risk of serious head injury?

Varying by the continuum of risk, some riders go without a helmet because they can easily cost $100. Some may prefer a helmet, but it is sadly unaffordable. At the other end of the scale, many riders see helmets as an uncool diminution of their stylistic expression. One exemplary New York messenger who has suffered from five concussions in his 15 years of riding doesn't wear a helmet (Staff 2002). Another messenger, in Boston, argued that it was "inconvenient" and was "just too much stuff around your head" (Staff 2002). Just days after the 2005 CMWC in New York, one participant from Oregon was involved in an accident in Manhattan's SoHo neighborhood. He was riding through an intersection in typical messenger fashion—he had seen his line and was floating through traffic against a red light. He intended to go behind a car that was crossing the intersection in front of him, but the driver saw him and reflexively slammed on his brakes. The rider "T-boned" the car and was launched over the trunk and into the street, landing on his head. He was not wearing a helmet, and suffered serious brain injuries and memory loss. Somehow unwilling to learn from this lesson, most of the messengers who rode to visit him in the hospital did not wear helmets either. When asked about this obvious incongruity, some messengers spun elaborate justifications involving the citation of dubious studies that purport to show that the helmeted rider is more likely to break her neck than the un-helmeted rider. While it is true that wearing a helmet very slightly increases the likelihood of neck injuries, this risk is far outweighed by the reduction of injuries to the skull and brain. Scholars have estimated that helmets could reduce up to 85 percent of cycling fatalities that are due to head injuries (Attewell et al 2001, Li and Baker 1997, Noakes 1995).

A recent law (effective July 2007) in New York City requires employers to provide helmets for bicycle delivery employees, including independent contractors. The messenger community reacted quite strongly. Many decried the obvious contradiction that ICs are not employees for tax purposes, but they are considered employees for the purposes of social control. Others had disparaging comments for legislators: "Please stop trying to protect me from myself" one said. Still others took a humorous angle, asking if an IC, being technically self-employed would have to sue himself if he did not provide himself with a helmet. But by far the strongest criticism against the helmet law came in the form of indignation at being told what to do. Interestingly some messengers realized that the issue of posengers could cut both ways:

> This is a good time to start poseing as fakengers, so not to get a real "messenger" ticket. "Why no officer, I am just in a real big hurry to get to a Starbucks patio. Of course I'm not a real messenger."

Instead of non-messengers posing as messengers in order to cash in on the cultural capital of messenger-chic, messengers themselves could claim to be fakengers in order to avoid a ticket. This is an amazingly adept identity-based slight of hand: a messenger posing as a citizen posing as a messenger.

Why value style over safety? For some, it is not style so much as expense. But for others, the image and identity of being a messenger simply doesn't overlap with wearing a helmet: helmets are just uncool. Others make a questionable safety argument. And still others claim inconvenience due to their headphones, hats, or sunglasses. In sum, for many messengers style wins over rationality and safety. But regardless of a rider's justifications, there are some forms of irrationality that couriers cannot escape, such as the inattentive driver or the frustrated road-rager.

Road raging drivers are not the most common source of injury for messengers—that honor goes to being "doored" by a driver who carelessly opens a car door into the bike lane. Injury can result from a courier smashing into the open door, or being hit by a car when the courier dodges into traffic to avoid the opened door. This can happen regardless of skill or ability, and it can happen without a messenger even realizing what was going on. A driver who opens her door without looking, just as a rider is passing, can hit the rider's rear wheel, knocking her over without the rider ever seeing the door or the driver. The bike messenger faces injuries and risk in every moment passing a parked car, at every intersection, and during most moments in between.

Though uncommon, road rage is by far the most dangerous situation that messengers face. The paradigmatic case occurred on 26 April 1999, a rainy day in Chicago. The driver of an SUV, Carnell Fitzpatrick, had an altercation with a messenger named Tommy McBride. It started when McBride slapped the hood of Fitzpatrick's Chevy Tahoe. To McBride this was a normal gesture, used without malice or intended harm, to draw the driver's attention to the cyclist—most commonly to indicate that the driver was squeezing the rider into a line of parked cars. To Fitzpatrick, however, this was an invasion of his extended personal space. Enraged, Fitzpatrick chased McBride through the streets, gunning his motor and tapping McBride's rear wheel with his bumper. After several bumps, McBride went down and fell under the SUV. Fitzpatrick kept driving, pausing a block away to dislodge McBride's bicycle from his bumper. Fitzpatrick later turned himself in to the police after realizing that his front license plate was sheared off in the accident and was left at the scene, tangled up in the wreckage of the bicycle and rider. Fitzpatrick was found guilty of first-degree murder and sentenced to 45 years in prison (Culley 2001: 294-96; Sadovi 2002).

Messengers are wary of their interactions with drivers because they know that road rage can come at any place or time. Many couriers react strongly to drivers who put the couriers' lives in danger, as well as to police officers who seem to enforce laws against cyclists while routinely letting drivers go for infractions that could be fatal to couriers. At the speed of traffic, a simple lapse on the part of a driver—like forgetting to use a turn indicator or opening a door without looking—could cause a cyclist to go down.

And yet road rage in drivers has an analog in cyclists, often expressed by swinging the ubiquitous U-lock that messengers use to secure their bikes. As one messenger said:

> i don't recall askin' for the cops to fuck with me or anybody else but that's the way things are and as long as i have to use my ulock or some language that may offend to get yours or anybody else's attention who is endangering my life then that's what i'll do. do i want or like havin' to yell to avoid being hit every day? no but i do not want to die.

This is a typical—if strongly worded—response to the continual threat of injury posed to messengers. But some couriers notice the irony of an enraged response to inattentive drivers or oblivious pedestrians:

> Someone . . . compared the clueless ped to the asshole driving the bmw. I would go so far as to compare the shoulder-checking courier to the asshole in the bmw.

Messengers, however, have shown an uncanny awareness that they are seen as both professionals and vermin on wheels, and many have come to understand that a reaction of "smile and wish them a nice day" is as effective as the angry response of yelling, spitting, slapping the hood, or smashing a wing-mirror with a U-lock. One messenger, on the topic of commuters who think they "own" the road, said:

> Your average driver/commuter, more often than not, seems to be bent on letting the lowly cyclist know that driving a car is much more prestigious, and therefore we have no right to impede their otherwise efficient mode of transportation. Run ins are common and while I have resorted to lock-swinging, spitting, car-smacking, this usually only serves to get said motorist even more enraged, where-upon it becomes open season. My methods have changed over the years and now find there is nothing more satisfying then just smiling and waving at the offending motorists. This may seem like a tame response to someone playing with your life with their vehicle, but most of these people have boring mundane lives and messing with you and getting an angry reaction is what makes their day.

This messenger has grown to understand that avoidance of conflict is the best way to preserve his life and continue his job. Getting into an altercation not only is a losing proposition given the difference in power and weight between a car and a bicycle, it also means that the messenger loses money.

Messengers express a larger sense of community, as well. Many couriers understood, if implicitly, that collective action matters a great deal, and that commuters were likely to encounter other messengers on subsequent days. This messenger went on:

> Spitting in someone's face or taking off their rear-view with your
> lock feels REALLY good the split second you do it but keep in mind,
> the next time this motorist has a incident with a cyclist/messenger,
> they will remember "the last time" and said cyclist may not be fortu-
> nate enough to get away from his/her assailant. Most cities with a
> messenger community want people to look at them as professionals.
> When people witness lock-swinging or spitting etc. it only re-
> enforces the negative stereotype of the Bicycle Messenger. Do your-
> self and others a favor and don't give Joe Public any more fuel for
> their already twisted idea of what Bicycle Messengers are about.

By dealing with road rage in a calculated manner—appreciating the
potential consequences of letting their own rage overtake them—most
messengers show a savvy understanding of their marginal space and how
to protect it and themselves. One creative messenger reported that his
method of recording pertinent information yielded an especially good
response:

> One thing I've done . . . is to pull out a piece of paper so they can see
> me right down their license plate #'s and other details, while smiling
> satisfyingly, causing them to think you'll report them to a driver
> compliance office or something. A few results: One guy let out a de-
> featist wail, one guy turned lily white and made apologetic faces at
> me.

Another courier, who owns the only messenger company in town, had
this to say about defending cyclists' rights with U-locks:

> In [my town], if a courier put a ulock through a driver's window, [my
> company] would be outta biz so fast you'd think we'd wanted it that
> way. Town's too small for shit like that. Doesn't mean we've got
> nice, polite folks to deal with, no sirree. We've got aldermen in the
> area who run cyclists off the road. We've got drunk fratboys & road
> rage & all the rest of it. One U-lock incident like that . . . I cringe. I
> carry one, mind you, & I've no qualms about using it if the situation
> sunk THAT low. But believe me, I'd need many witnesses & a DAMN
> good reason. You can't just bolt off here & say, Oh it musta been an-
> other courier company. [We are] it. Makes us creative.

Creative responses to road rage and the threat of physical violence
have earned the respect of many, police officers included. Though messengers routinely disregard traffic laws (going the wrong way down one
way streets, riding through turn lanes, ignoring stop signs and lights), it
is interesting to note that many report interactions with police as generally reasonable. Though police often harass the "Critical Mass" rides,
when a single rider has an interaction with a police officer it is often
civil. One messenger explained it thus:

> Having been a Messenger for many years, I have had my share of
> run-ins with our local constabulary. I have found that if you are "just
> one person" they will usually let you off with a warning. Dog help

> you if you are on a critical mass ride here as this sense of organiza-
> tion seems to get the local fuzz's knickers in a major twist.

This courier's comment uncovers how traffic laws are really enforced, and how the ruling relations of law and discretion unfold in the city streets. Many police officers know that messengers perform an important service to businesses and the local government. Only when violations are outrageous or when the sense of individuals organizing for political change (as with Critical Mass, discussed in more detail in Chapter 5) will police crack down on messengers. Though police will, at times, delay messengers for violating the vehicle code, this—as with most law en-forcement—is highly dependent upon public pressure. From time-to-time there is a media outcry about messengers, and the police step up their enforcement of laws governing bicycles. In fact, in some cities a mes-senger's first ticket is seen as a rite of passage, some even brag about how many tickets they have collected. Predictably, there is also the occa-sional contest between cops and messengers. Many couriers proudly related stories to me about a cop who tried to pull them over, but the messenger simply disappeared into traffic the wrong way down a one-way street, with the police unable or unwilling to pursue in their car. Still other couriers lament the rise of police on bikes (derisively called "cop-sicles"). Though couriers can usually still outrun them, many bike cops see it as their bailiwick to enforce the law that governs all bike riders in the city, especially messengers. But in general, in the absence of public outcry over "those lunatic messengers," most police respect and are respected by messengers. Other professional drivers, however, offer a different story.

People come to feel ownership over places and identify strong emo-tions with particular locations. This might be the neighborhood where someone grew up or the scene of a memorable experience. It is some-times simple nostalgia, but it is also true of people who work in a par-ticular location for a period of time. Office workers might personalize their cubicle with photos and knickknacks. Air force pilots have a tradi-tion of painting images on the noses of their planes. Some people name their cars. This is a way of personalizing the impersonal, of adding a human touch to an alienating environment.

Those who work the streets are no different. Delivery professionals of all types often develop a sense of propriety over the streets as part of an identity that is born from long-time experience. And this feeling of connection and ownership can be a powerful emotion: one messenger I worked with used to yell at drivers who cut him off "I OWN these streets!" Competition on the road sometimes means that cab drivers and bus drivers joust with messengers. Of course the size and acceleration difference between cyclists and drivers makes this an extremely unequal power relation. But drivers have their understandings of who owns the streets, and it usually does not include cyclists. Messengers, on the other hand, have some imagined parameters of acceptable behavior on the part of professional drivers. If cabbies or bus drivers cross that line, messengers have been known to take some underhanded revenge.

One Chicago messenger told me about a duel he had with a bus driver near the end of a shift. The bus was an oversized coach with an accordion joint in the middle. This lumbering beast was slow to accelerate, and had to stop every two blocks to load and unload riders. The messenger could easily stay ahead of the bus in traffic, but the driver insisted on gunning his motor to pass the courier, watching the bike rider in his rear-view mirror, and then cutting him off at each bus stop. It was the courier's opinion that the driver was doing this intentionally just to be annoying and to prove his supposed superiority. After several instances, the courier got fed up, pulled out his U-lock, and smashed the wing mirror of the bus. Chicago law dictates certain safety requirements, and the bus driver had to stop the bus, unload his passengers, and wait for a new bus to come. Was this courier justified in his reaction? Perhaps he was not, as he certainly caused significant delay for many passengers on that bus. But the bus driver, one hopes, learned a certain "David versus Goliath" lesson as well.

One run-in with a bus driver when I was on shift is emblematic of the ownership that many drivers feel about the streets. The street was narrow, with only two tight lanes and guardrails to keep pedestrians from jaywalking. Just past an intersection, a bus pulled to the side, directly beneath a "no parking anytime" sign. At precisely the moment I came up behind the parked bus another bus coming from the opposite direction pulled up parallel. I was in a rush, and could not hop the curb due to the guardrail. Since there was no getting around the bus on the right side, I was forced to ride the centerline between the two busses, ducking underneath the wing mirror. Just as I was emerging from this odd vehicular canyon, the bus driver who had illegally parked came walking in front of his bus, jaywalking to a convenience store across the street. I hit him square on, knocking him down. The convenience store owner came running out and joined the bus driver in yelling at me for some perceived infraction. Apparently bus drivers own the street, can flagrantly violate several laws at once, and then blame others for their own stupidity.

But as with the police, altercations with bus drivers are fewer than one might imagine. Cab drivers, on the other hand, are almost universally reviled by messengers, perhaps because they, too, must cross town with alacrity. Not only do cabbies pose a serious danger to cyclists when they dodge to the curb to pick up a fare, but in some cities they compete directly with bike couriers by delivering packages when paying passengers are fewer in the middle of the day. This competition, in some cities, has bled over into outright animosity. There are stories (possibly apocryphal) of messengers who keep two water bottles on their bike frames—one for drinking water and the other to urinate in. This second bottle becomes ammunition against unruly cab drivers. No doubt this simply stokes the fires and escalates the war.

One courier told me about his creative and disarming approach to defusing such battles. As the courier rode through heavy traffic, a cabbie intentionally cut him off by partially changing from the left to the right lane, blocking the space between lanes that the courier was traversing. The messenger threaded through traffic to go into the curb lane, and the cabbie continued forward at an angle to block that area too. When the courier hopped the curb and continued on his way, the cabbie blasted his horn and gestured rudely. Several blocks up the cabbie passed the messenger, pulling close to him and squeezing him towards the parked cars. Luckily the messenger slowed and avoided any injury. At a stop light after another block the messenger caught up with the cab driver, who rolled down his window. Just as he was about to blast the courier with some obscenities, the courier looked at him quizzically and asked: "Excuse me sir, are you wearing pants?" The confused cabbie looked down into his lap, and the messenger rolled away through the red light, leaving the chagrinned cabbie behind. This non-combative, de-escalating approach shows a presence of mind on the part of the messenger, but also shows a certain amount of prudence.

These incidents and stories show several interlocking dynamics involved in messenger work. First, they show the sort of specialized knowledge and creative approaches that messengers develop over time. They might be prepared to wage war if needed, but they also know how to take a disarming approach. Many of the fastest messengers do not get worked up over perceived slights or aggression from other drivers. Of course its understandable if they do, since it involves their lives, not just a scratch in the taxi's paint. These creative responses are also a negotiation of risk. By behaving in a disarming way during potentially violent situations, messengers can reduce their vulnerability and get on with their jobs. By diffusing danger and managing risk couriers can focus on getting the job done.

Overall, most couriers are cognizant of the effect that their actions have on other cyclists, and they also understand how their image is presented to customers, pedestrians, and police. Most work hard to be professional and courteous, while doing their job as quickly as possible:

> I myself think that most customers respect me, because I keep their business going, I transport things as fast as possible, and sometimes even impossible, therefore they admire me. My bike and my clothes are clean and on the road and especially in pedestrian areas I try to be fast but polite, because I represent a company and every man on the street is a possible customer.

Many messengers have a keen understanding of their multiple roles as individual worker, representative of an image-conscious company, and symbol of the larger group of bicycle messengers. They learn how to navigate these conflicting identities to manage both image and risk.

One innovative solution to the combination of the risky character of the occupation and its economic marginalization in regards to health care is the Bicycle Messenger Emergency Fund (BMEF), started by an enterprising and civic-minded former messenger. In the style of a classic benevolent association, this fund gathers donations from messengers to support couriers who have suffered accidents. The small amount (usually $400 or so) is meant to carry a messenger through for a week or two in the event that they are unable to work, cannot cover medical bills, etc. As the organizer of the BMEF put it:

> The BMEF has been set up to assist bicycle messengers who have been injured while working. The current time consideration for consideration of an injury is within the past couple of days. Not exceeding a week from injury. This fund isn't an insurance policy for workers comp or disability insurance. This was decided to prevent payout to long-term injuries that continue to be part of any bicycle messenger's life on the road. The whole idea is to get emergency cash to a messenger when they can't even get out of bed or walk to the bathroom from severe pain. They need food and pain medicine.

There is some debate in the messenger community about payback to the BMEF. Many think that couriers with the ability to replenish the fund should do so. Many have, and still more have organized benefit races, or donated their winnings from races. The difficulty of verifying repayment to the fund, however, has prevented any rules from solidifying.

The BMEF in many ways exemplifies the larger messenger community. It is self-organized, informal, and solves the problem of economic marginalization without challenging the larger economic system. As one courier noted:

> There is something uniquely utopian about a program where messengers all over the world work to help each other in times of need. A lasting and successful BMEF . . . would be a huge accomplishment for the entire messenger community.

Utopian indeed. Mutual benevolence associations have tried to mitigate the savageries of capitalism for at least 200 years in the US. They offer a way to serve the specific needs of workers without relying on the state or the good will of the bosses. But the BMEF also symbolizes the do it yourself attitude, solidarity, and co-operation of the global messenger community.[5]

Conclusion

Messengers are marginal in their employment conditions. They get paid on a piece-rate system that forces them to engage in risky behavior in an already dangerous job. They do not generally receive health care or other benefits, and are not generally unionized. And yet they voluntarily take risks and manage the emotional processes associated with dangerous occupations both as individuals and as a group. Part of this process is to cognitively minimize the notion of risk, partially by constructing it as banal, and partly by valorizing risk. What constitutes risky behavior is in the eye of the beholder, and messengers in some ways treat risk as just part of the job, something that comes with the territory. In this, they are classic edgeworkers, inhabiting varying locations on the continuum of risk, from voluntary to economically co-erced. But in managing this risk they make it an issue of coping ability, emphasizing a masculinized skill in handling danger. They discuss risk in terms of exposure time, taking pride in their ability to make it through the gauntlet of the city streets. But some couriers also deny the reality of risk, for example by refusing to wear a helmet. In part these are differing responses to the same social structural context, different sets of durable dispositions that assign cultural meaning to risk. Furthermore, the messenger community, as it has developed over the last 20 years, has produced a distinctive culture and special solidarity-building events, which help to navigate and mitigate the banality of risk.

Notes

1 A New York City messenger as quoted in *New York Times* 29 April 2007 "Unstoppable" by Jocko Weyland.

2. Giddens (2000) makes a similar argument, stressing the historical nature of the concept of risk. Risk as a specific western idea arose only with the primitive accumulation stage of capitalism and colonialism: sailing a ship across the ocean was a risky endeavor. This swash-buckling notion of daring-do was eventually extended to financial behavior and into everyday life. In the modern "runaway" world, risk is not necessarily less nor greater than in the past, but its character has moved from an individual level to a societal or global level. As with Beck, to Giddens ecological risk or the risk of nuclear holocaust is an abstract notion to be dealt with by experts, not individuals. The public must trust governments and scientists as technocrats—in Foucaultian terms, governmentality—and giving up this power to the experts makes the public further prone to mass control. Giddens calls for a public involvement with risk management to offset this centralization of power.

3. Working from Beck's framework, Mol and Spaargaren (1993, 2002) have shown how steps are now being undertaken at the firm level, at the sector level, and at the state and international levels to address global climate change, mitigate its worst effects, and lower the carbon loading of the atmosphere: risk has now been recognized, reflected upon, and addressed in policy (though perhaps less effectively than one might hope for).

4. Often the mobilization of aggression is a heavily masculine trait, rarely exhibited by female couriers, as discussed in chapter 4.

5. The author's proceeds from this book will be donated to the Bicycle Messenger Emergency Fund.

4. Visibility and Invisibility: Liminality, Anarchy, and Bike-Punk Culture

"Being a messenger is not about dodging things, or swearing at cops or people who are in your way, it's about being invisible, so you don't HAVE to dodge and swear."[1]

Messengers occupy a contradictory location in the city: they are both supremely visible as a symbol of urban culture and yet the effective courier is invisible to cars, pedestrians, and traffic. Just as janitors, garbage haulers, and dishwashers do the work many don't want to, messengers are little seen but greatly necessary to the smooth functioning of our modern urban areas. Not only do messengers occupy a physically marginal space in the street, they inhabit a liminal realm where they are ubiquitous but invisible, symbolic yet ordinary. They cross boundaries between work and play, between reverence and derogation, between maintaining capitalism and rebelling against it. They are heroes and lunatics, either/or, both and neither.

Hero, Anti-hero, or Lunatic? Messengers in their (un)natural habitat

In delivering packages in a busy downtown core, messengers deal with many obstacles, from oblivious pedestrians (called "peds" or "suits"), to road-raging commuters, to hostile cabbies and bus drivers.

Bicycle messengers see these peds, cabs and cars as obstacles to a speedy delivery. And so they weave through the streets, often breaking laws but rarely breaking bones. The media call them "grungy," "free-spirited," "daredevils," or even "agents of Satan" (Freeman 2004; King and Van Praet 2004; Martin 1998). From the character played by Kevin Bacon in the 1986 film "Quicksilver" to the scruffy courier depicted in television commercials, the bicycle messenger is seen variously as hero of the city (for the feats of athleticism in getting the job done) and anti-hero (for the sweaty, greasy, unkempt appearance and the illegal traffic maneuvers). Appreciative or not, those on the street often see messengers as lunatics on wheels.

The messenger sees a completely different reality. The street from a messenger's view is constantly changing; dangers rising and falling with each stroke of the pedals. A courier cannot insulate herself from the street the way a car driver can roll up his window—the sights and smells and grit of the street are ever-present for the messenger. As described by Lynn Breedlove (2002: 3) in her account of messengering in San Francisco:

> You're breathing bus fumes and spices from restaurants and charred
> fish and raw sewage, and then you got cabs and buses whizzing in
> and out of the corner of your eye.

The constant barrage of sensory information is what messengers have to overcome in order to deliver packages on time—the only thing they are paid to do. In the midst of traffic the messenger must both pay careful attention and filter out information on a continual basis: they must watch for the cars changing lanes, the cabbies swerving to pick up a fare, the sewer grates, and even other messengers. But they must simultaneously ignore all of the superfluous stimulation that takes up so much of public space: the billboards, the sounds, and the smells. Navigating the streets demands a hyper-awareness that can sometimes lead messengers to feel as if they know what is going to happen before it actually does. By ignoring other stimuli and paying attention to the cues of drivers, messengers can move around obstacles before they even get in the way. One messenger in Spain told me:

> Once you're already used to the noise of traffic and used to riding
> fast and close, there's not a whole lot that can distract you—not the
> taxicabs or the mopeds in your armpit, not the potholes, not even a
> grandmother jaywalking while pushing a stroller with an infant . . .
> and I don't even get upset with idiots in traffic because I knew they
> were going to be idiots and how they were going to be idiots, and I
> am already out of harm's way.

It is part prophesy, part awareness, and part luck. And this complex calculation of seeing, hearing, feeling, and ignoring unimportant details all happen at 20 miles per hour in cramped city streets.

The two main barriers to timely delivery are traffic (autos and pedestrians) and traffic signals. Car traffic and signals can be managed because they are relatively predictable. Pedestrians are more difficult because they can be highly unpredictable. One courier summarized the problem as "blind Christmas shoppers looking the wrong way down the street as they walk out under your wheels." Car drivers may honk, curse, or shake their fist at a messenger, but pedestrians don't seem to pay attention to anything:

> so the light a 1/4 mile up has just turned green {4 me} i get up to about 14-15 miles per/hr and the peds are on the edge of the sidewalk and start to walk out into street. Of course, not wanting to get hit by or hit a ped i yell "don't walk" which in every city I've ridden in prior, people don't walk or they stop as I'm going pretty fast and i have the green. NOT HERE!!! THOSE FU**ING ASSHOLES WALK RIGHT INTO ME. I of course had to stop on that green light to avoid hitting those pricks and if i hadn't stopped i would be in jail after my trip to the hospital.

Many messengers I talked to had more creative approaches than simply yelling since most pedestrians today are plugged into an ipod or yakking on a cell phone. One courier suggested a coach's whistle to grab attention, and another joked that "whistles are for rookies. I hear that the 30 foot shooting taser works really well, but you then have to bunny-hop their writhing bodies." Some messengers felt strongly enough to suggest physical action, including shoulder-checking, or intentionally hitting pedestrians:

> I know most bikers have strong legs and small shoulders, but grow some tough shoulders and put them into a few pedestrians. Make absolutely certain all of your momentum and force goes into the jaywalker. If you are going to make the first hit, make it a good one. Better to hit the pedestrian than the asphalt. It is not nice to do, but it is the best way to survive in the long run.

In some ways this is a comment on living in a dense urban environment. The masses in the way of messengers on a daily basis mean that pedestrians become *obstacles* instead of *people*.

This is a process of dehumanization, and it is part of the human condition. People differentiate others into categories: some are accepted into the group while others are excluded. Processes of in-group/out-group distinctions are common to all societies. Durkheim called this social solidarity (Durkheim 1984 [1893]), and elaborated on how it can be found even in ancient animist religious societies (Durkheim 1995 [1912]). We experience solidarity with others based on mutual experiences (mechanical solidarity) or mutual need (organic solidarity). Those who we do not think that we need, or who do not share our experience are likely to be seen as outsiders. Group status is often reflected in language. Couriers call pedestrians "peds" or "suits." In war we call the enemy by derogatory labels to ease the psychological weight of killing. Racist, sexist, and homophobic epithets serve a similar function, often with violent results. As messengers dehumanize pedestrians, violence becomes more likely, evidenced by the above suggestion of shoulder-checking jaywalking peds. And yet there are many messengers who recoil at such suggestions and strive to peacefully coexist with traffic. The best solution, many couriers find, is to avoid pedestrians entirely, especially during periods of heavy downtown shopping, near the University, or a central square. In high pedestrian-traffic areas messengers get slowed down and may have to take other risks to make the delivery on time.

As discussed in the previous chapter, in order to make a living wage (or to complete a rush delivery on time) it is often necessary for messengers to run lights. The challenge is to do so without getting crushed. Catching the tail-end of a yellow light is easy to do safely. Couriers learn to calculate the time they have to get across the intersection before cross-traffic enters the intersection. Many lights have a built-in delay and it takes some time for the drivers to register that their light has turned. This extra time allows a courier to "stretch" a yellow light while not having to risk being broadsided. Clearly this is not only illegal, but dangerous. Drivers may "jump" the light or a car may be approaching the intersection at speed rather than starting from a dead halt. But "stretching a yellow" is far less risky than running a light that has been red for some time.

Actually blowing through a red light is something that many couriers do as a matter of course. "Floating an intersection," as it is called, is like a three-dimensional real-life version of the video game "Frogger." Defying common sense, messengers will run a red light and weave through cross-traffic. Floating an intersection is half art and half insanity. A great deal of skill is involved, and clearly the stakes are quite high. Couriers quickly learn what speeds you need, what maneuverability you can manage, and how drivers will react. The approach is to "pick a line" based on a set of assumptions: that drivers will generally continue obliviously on their course, that pedestrians will usually freeze in place if they see you, and that the rider will be able to dodge here and there as needed. Rather than individual cars, the cross-traffic becomes a singular thing that has holes in it: elastic gaps in the flow. The key is to see these gaps as opportunities, and to exploit them by threading a line through each gap, jumping from one to another seamlessly the way that Frogger jumps from log to lily pad. Cross-traffic is just another barrier between the rider and the destination.

A courier can be seen as a sociopathic anti-hero darting through traffic and flaunting laws, but really he is just trying to beat the cross-town traffic and get the package delivered on time. The reputation as urban cowboy is one that many messengers enjoy, while others abhor it. Messengers see themselves as many things, including all of the stereotypes above. One messenger from Germany expresses the most common view:

> In my opinion bike messengers neither are heroes, nor asphalt-cowboys or whatever they are described as. This does not mean, that this job is no fun and it does not push your adrenalin, but in the first place it is a service and it is sport.

Messengers can be hero, anti-hero, lunatic, and athlete. They move in between these labels and personify a shifting terrain of meaning. Couriers broadly understand these meanings and identities, but how to deal with the imposition of meaning is the subject of intense debate in the community. Many couriers, when faced with an irate driver about to enter road-rage, will resort to their own form of intimidation, including physical coercion. The mismatch between a bike rider and a car driver in size, power, and lethal force might seem obvious. But most cars become an extension of the driver's personal space. Cars are a bubble of private space in the public space of the street, an insulating privilege bicycle riders do not enjoy. Threatening this private and personal space by slapping an open hand on their car, or brandishing a formidable object like a U-lock, is enough to make many drivers back down. Yet these same actions may further enrage others:

> Your average driver/commuter, more often than not, seems to be bent on letting the lowly cyclist know that driving a car is much more prestigious, and therefore we have no right to impede their otherwise efficient mode of transportation. Run-ins are common and while I have resorted to lock-swinging, spitting, car-smacking, this usually only serves to get said motorist even more enraged, where-upon it becomes open season.

This courier explained how his methods have changed over time to become more subtle. He now smiles, waves, and avoids getting angry. Messengers who have been around a while are generally a bit more aware of the larger messenger community, and thus express a more mature and reasoned perspective such as the above. Others cannot afford to take on such an identity as rebel or scofflaw. Embracing the identity of the professional, courteous messenger can be difficult in the face of lack of approval from one's peers.

Like floating through traffic, the shifting terrain of meanings that messengers navigate gives them a liminal character: they are dirty, smelly low-life, yet also clean, efficient professionals. They are both and neither, they are either/or.

Liminality: city space and bicycle messengers

Victor Turner developed the concepts of liminality and liminal space to characterize rituals of transition (Turner 1967; Turner 1974; Turner 1982). Bike messengers inhabit both a physically marginal and a sym-bolically liminal realm.[2] Liminality, according to Turner, can convey a special status in society.

The metaphor of liminality as Turner describes it applies to "transi-tional beings" that have a "liminal persona." The subject of a liminal period or process is structurally, if not physically, "invisible" (1967: 95). Building from van Gennep's (1960 [1908]) notion of the rites of passage, Turner argued that liminal beings are *somewhere in between*, they are neither one category nor another. Somehow they occupy both at the same time. As transitional beings deny category, they also deny hierarchy. And so it is with bicycle messengers: "she came out of nowhere," says the driver who strikes a cyclist with his car; "he disappeared into the traffic," says the irate cop trying to find a red-light running messenger. As one messenger described the neophytes who yell and weave in and out of traffic (also printed as the epigram to this chapter):

being a messenger is not about dodging things, or swearing at cops or
people who are in your way, it's about being invisible, so you don't
HAVE to dodge and swear.

Invisibility allows a messenger to pass through the city and avoid the pitfalls of traffic. As they navigate the physical margins of the street messengers become symbolically liminal characters.

Urban planners in the last 50 years have primarily considered cars and pedestrians when designing cities and passing traffic laws. Bicycle messengers are neither, they are somewhere in between. Though they can often deliver a package faster than an auto, there are clear advantages of speed, acceleration, and weight in a car. Yet cyclists have the same ad-vantages over pedestrians. This is the uneasy harmony that messengers represent on so many levels: "This coincidence of opposite processes and notions in a single representation characterizes the particular unity of the liminal: that which is neither this nor that, and yet is both" (Turner 1967: 99).

Messengers also blur the boundaries between work and sport, as the courier above noted. In discussing liminality Turner notes that "play" can also be serious (1982: 30-39). In western cultures the bike is a symbol of youthful playfulness. It is not something that grown men and women use for work—except perhaps as an athletic tool in sport cycling. But bicycle messengers take the child's toy and modify it for gainful employment.

The fact that messenger work is both serious and playful challenges some of the distinctions that sociologists have made about occupations and workers. Durkheim (1984 [1893], 1995 [1912]), for instance, notes that in modern society we are drudgingly forced into occupations, and the moments of freedom during leisure time are the places where we can experience collective effervescence. While this may be true for many workers, it rings false for messengers. Bicycle couriers, in some ways, get to play all day on their bikes. It is common to see messengers grimacing with the efforts and focus of their work, but it is just as common to see them grinning and high-fiving each other as they pass on the streets. The play aspect, and the resulting collective effervescence is also emphasized in messenger gatherings when off-duty. But there is an element of play in much of a courier's day; he blurs the lines, existing somewhere in between.

The characteristics of liminal groups include tolerance and a lack of structure. They are often a "community or comity of comrades and not a structure of hierarchically arrayed positions. This comradeship transcends distinctions of rank, age, kinship position, and, in some kinds of cultic groups, even sex" (1967: 100). Bicycle messengers often take pride at the tolerance and anti-structure that their community possesses. Those who are attracted to messengering as a profession often express as an ideal the non-hierarchical organization, as exemplified by Alley Cats races and Critical Mass demonstrations, described in Chapter 5. Couriers sometimes bristle at the direct orders that come from authoritarian dispatchers, or at police, cabbies, or pedestrians. This strong anti-hierarchical perspective has roots in punk rock culture and the political theory of anarchism.

God save the queen: bike messengers and punk rock

Bike messengers and punk rock are curiously related. Messengers are certainly a fierce bunch. Many are quite adamantly opposed to capitalism, organized religion, and hierarchical government. There is a great deal of overlap between the community of messengers and the punk rock community in this and in other respects. One courier from Ireland told me that bike messengers belonged to a "dynamic, vibrant punk rock subculture." What is punk? And why do bike messengers seem so closely aligned with punk culture, punk rock music, and anti-establishment styles?

The most important early work on punk culture, a defining work of cultural studies, is Dick Hebdige's *Subculture: The Meaning of Style*. According to Hebdige, subcultures[3] form in communal and symbolic engagements with the larger system of late industrial culture. Subcultures are often organized around age or class, and are expressed in the creation of styles. Such forms of stylistic expression are produced by particular groups in specific historical and cultural conjunctures along lines of race, class, age and other fractures of society. People create a subcultural style by adopting hybrid images and various bits of material culture. Out of these pieces they can construct a relatively autonomous identity within the broader social order. As punks did in the late 1970s, so too do bike messengers hyrbidize styles and culture to produce a new subcultural identity.

Clothes in a hybridized, subcultural style are often homemade, altered, manipulated, or worn with a sense of irony: Johnny Rotten, lead singer of the Sex Pistols, famously wore a t-shirt with "I hate" scrawled above a graphic for the band Pink Floyd. Punks wore dirty clothes held together with safety pins. Ripped outfits were a badge of disaffection and distance from the establishment. But importantly, this resultant hybrid style is not immune from co-optation: commercial culture appropriates and even produces counter-hegemonic styles in a continual evolution of fad and fashion. Indeed, some suggest that the Sex Pistols, godfathers of punk, were essentially "sell outs" from the beginning.[4] But punk style exploded into a subcultural phenomenon and is not just a "rock n' roll swindle." While punk mixed an avant-garde cultural strategy with working-class transgression and estrangement from traditional consumer markets, this became co-opted and commercialized: punk style clothes are now available at "Hot Topic" in your local shopping mall. Many bike messengers have adopted clothing reminiscent of punks, crossed with some aspects of sport-cycling's technical gear. They often use special-ized track racing bikes, outfitted to the rigors of street riding. And of course, today anyone can buy clothes and bikes like the messengers developed at local cycling shops. And so the line between subculture as resistance and the commercialization and co-optation of subculture can be thin: what was once a statement of resistance can become an instru-ment of capitalist hegemony.

In regards to punk, Hebdige argues that subculture is a symbolic form of resistance to hegemonic ideals. Punk famously told the estab-lishment to "fuck off"—all of the establishment, that is, from economic and political elites to the cultural purveyors of fad and fashion. Punk music combined elements of glam-rock, R&B, reggae, and the American underground rock music of the Velvet Underground, Iggy Pop, and the Ramones; it was nihilistic, with an emphasis on simplicity and minimal-ism. As Hebdige puns, this "unlikely alliance of diverse and superficially incompatible musical traditions" was "literally safety-pinned together" (1980: 26).

But contradictions abound in this subcultural bricolage. Some strands of punk culture were homophobic, racist, or sexist. Some punks sported swastikas on their beat up leather jackets as a strong symbol of rebellion, and yet the music was heavily influenced by reggae and other imports of the black British working class. Many punks held homophobic postures, yet the etymology of the term "punk" relates to male-male sex, and is still used in African American culture and elsewhere as a derisive term for homosexuals. And while many punks and messengers adhere to an anarchistic political philosophy of self-organization, hierarchies are reproduced: if your clothes aren't dirty enough, or your hair is not spiky enough, or your bike doesn't quite fit the bill, you may well be judged unworthy.

Contradictions notwithstanding, punk culture has historically devel-oped against any hierarchies or categories. Marc Bayard, in trying (not) to define punk, says: "Punk has made the explicit aim of trying to destroy all boxes and labels . . . any project that tries to define punk or explain it must do so with very broad brush strokes. Punk and punk music cannot be pigeonholed to some spiked-haired white male wearing a leather jacket with a thousand metal spikes listening to music real loud" (O'Hara 1999: 12). Nonetheless, we must attempt to define—or at least contextu-alize—punk within the twentieth century.

If Hebdige calls punk a symbolic form of resistance that, in typical DIY (Do It Yourself) fashion, fused multiple musical styles and used the body as a place of stylistic expression, Greil Marcus locates the secret roots of punk in the dada movements of 50 years before. Marcus writes that, like dada, "Punk immediately discredited the music that preceded it; punk denied the legitimacy of anyone who'd ever had a hit, or played as if he knew how to play. Destroying one tradition, punk revealed a new one" (Marcus 1990: 39). Punk was a negation in the Frankfurt School sense (Marcus 1990: 67):

> There was a reversal of perspective, of values: a sense that anything was possible, a truth that could be proven only in the negative. What had been good—love, money, and health—was now bad; what had been bad—hate, mendacity, and disease—was now good. The equations ran on, replacing work with sloth, status with reprobation, fame with infamy, celebrity with obscurity, professionalism with ignorance, civility with insult, nimble fingers with club feet, and the equations were unstable. In this new world where suicide was suddenly a code word for meaning what you said, nothing could be more hip than a corpse.

One might even say an exquisite corpse. Punk divided its adherents from society much as other subcultures do: the old were not to be trusted, the rich were to be abused, and life was to be lived fast (in Johnny Rotten's words, "no future / no future for me"). The instrumentation of punk made sense as a rejection of the establishment: it was loud, brash, and often anti-melodic. It was fast and jerky and the lyrics were shouted and spat out at the audience: Johnny Rotten might be the only person in the world who can make the lyrics "anarchy" and "UK" rhyme.

If there is a philosophy behind this stylistic musical rejection, it might be Do It Yourself. This is exemplified by the rejection of authority, market capitalism, and religion as organizing principles in favor of attempts to create a new system based on new values. "The driving ethic behind most sincere punk efforts is DIY . . . We don't need to rely on rich business men to organize our fun for their profit—we can do it ourselves for no profit" (Joel in *Profane Existence* #11/12 Autumn 1991 as quoted in O'Hara 1999: 153). DIY extends from fashion and stylistic expression to music production, distribution, and concert promotion. Messengering is in part an extension of such impulses. If there is one reason why many messengers embrace punk, it is because messengering is a simple, DIY way to make the rent without having to sell out to a desk job. But as discussed in some detail below, for the majority of messengers "punk" is just another word used to describe someone or something else. For these couriers it is just a job, not an expression of anything other than the need to pay bills.

What is utterly unpredicted from a traditional cultural studies perspective is how punk rock, as a critique of mass culture and commodification, came bursting out of popular culture itself. Punk was billed as a total rejection of what came before it, but it also blended elements of preceding music styles and philosophies into a new hybrid, a result that was then co-opted and commodified. Greil Marcus describes this process of rejection, reinvention, and commodification (Marcus 1990: 77):

> That was punk: a load of old ideas sensationalized into new feelings almost instantly turned into new clichés, but set forth with such momentum that the whole blew up its equations day by day. For every fake novelty there was a real one. For every third hand pose there was a fourth hand pose that turned into a real motive.

So punk is a bricolage of styles, musical genres, and ideas, all loaded up into the conjunctural moment of working-class London in 1977. It exploded onto the cultural scene and burned brightly and quickly—the Sex Pistols were the most visible symbol of punk from the first moments, and as a musical group they lasted less than a year. Writing of the Sex Pistols' last concert in San Francisco in January 1978 Marcus says (1990: 77):

> Punk was not a musical genre; it was a moment in time that took shape as a language anticipating its own destruction, and thus sometimes seeking it, seeking the statement of what could be said with neither words nor chords. It was not history. It was a chance to create ephemeral events that would serve as judgments on whatever came next, events that would judge all that followed wanting—that, too, was the meaning of no-future.

The nihilistic rejection of the boredom of mass society couldn't have a more pure expression than the un-helmeted bike messenger flying headfirst into traffic against a red light: "no future / no future for me." At a national race, one group of San Francisco messengers took the identity of bike punks to the extreme: they threw full cans of beer at one another, at nearby couriers, and even at racers on the course. Calling themselves the Chain-smokers,[5] these are athletes who smoke, drink, and do drugs while dressed in clothes reminiscent of the Hells Angels. Body piercings and tattoos abound. At one point they tossed their bikes into the cycling version of a mosh pit,[6] spray-painting them, torching them. Laughing at the whole idea of the race, one courier yelled: "Budweiser is my sports drink of choice!" After an abysmal showing in the qualifying round of a championship race, another said "maybe we should go into rehab so we can win some races."

This shows that punk continues: punk culture in similar forms still exists at the margins of society today. Though one can go to the mall and purchase a brand-new Sex Pistols t-shirt and a metal-studded black leather belt to hold up pre-ripped jeans, punk has persisted and resisted this commodification. Or perhaps phoenix-like it has risen from the ashes of 1977 and kept to the margins of society. Punk spaces still exist in unlikely warehouses such as the Gilman Street Project in Berkeley, in (illegal) housing squats in Minneapolis, in insurgent art spaces in New York, and in basement shows across the nation. Punk bands like Submission Hold and Propagandhi still rage against the establishment from independent record labels. Punk kids still astound their parents by shaving their hair into a spiky Mohawk. And in the bicycle messenger world this subculture is alive and well.

While Marcus writes that an end to punk was performed by the Sex Pistols in 1978, Craig O'Hara (1999: 71) and others point out that the 1980s was when punk blossomed into political consciousness:

> Bands such as Crass, Conflict, and Discharge in the UK, The Ex, and BGK in Holland, and MDC and the Dead Kennedys in America changed many Punks into rebellious thinkers rather than just Rock 'n' Rollers.

The line of this rebellious thought veered towards anarchism as a political philosophy instead of just a slogan. As the band Crass wrote in 1981 (as quoted in O'Hara 1999: 83):

> Anarchy is the only form of political thought that does not seek to control the individual through force . . . Anarchy is the rejection of that State control and represents a demand by the individual to live a life of personal choice, not one of political manipulation . . . By refusing to be controlled you are taking your own life into your own hands, and that is, rather than the popular idea of anarchy as chaos, the start of personal order . . . The state of anarchy is not a chaotic bedlam where everyone is out for themselves.

Anarchism has a bum rap in both mainstream and academic culture. In the common vernacular anarchy is synonymous with chaos. Yet anarchism as a political philosophy has been promulgated for more than 150 years, but always from a subaltern position *vis-à-vis* accepted political theory. Writers such as Pierre-Joseph Proudhon, Mikhail Bakunin, and Peter Kroptkin have suggested that anarchy is a mode of social organization that rejects religion, the capitalist market, and state power (Proudhon 2003 [1851], Bakunin 1971, Kropotkin 2002). Simplified under the slogan "no gods, no masters," anarchists often adhere to strict personal responsibility as a generalizable moral principle. As Mike Gunderloy, editor of *Factsheet Five* said in 1989: "I happen to believe that ends and means must be kept consistent. So lying, cheating, killing, and similar things are out as far as I'm concerned" (as quoted in O'Hara 1999: 88).

Such individual rectitude is a fundamental requirement for a self-organized community with no state, no bosses, no religious authorities, and no recognized leaders. This means "freedom from authority and rules; a place where people can live free from external compulsion. Thus police and even formalized laws would not be necessary" (O'Hara 1999: 95). But the preconditions for such an ideal community are not just individual responsibility and the smashing of capitalism and the state. Anarchism can also be thought of as a state of mind. Anarchy is not just the absence of laws but rather the absence of *the need* for the rule of law because people behave according to mutually accepted codes without the need for coercion. Such a community would realize Habermas' ideal of domination-free communication, Marx's ideal of "from each according to ability, to each according to need," and Durkheim's ideal of collective solidarity through group endeavors. A reflection of these ideals can be seen in the punk and messenger communities: from mutual assistance to a fierce emphasis on equality, anarchism is the principle of DIY in action.

At base, punk rock and bicycle messengering are overlapping communities at the margins of the established system that maintain themselves as a subcultural out-group through anti-hierarchical DIY techniques. Punk rock and bicycle messengering have an affinity because they are both communities at the margin of the system, but both reflect and reproduce significant aspects of the system that they rebel against.

And this begs a question about self-selection into the messenger industry. Do messengers become punks because they hate capitalism, or are they capitalism-hating punks first who take a messenger job because it fits their ethical position? As will be discussed further in Chapter 5, there is a division within messengers on the question of style. Some messengers adopt a punk demeanor and style as part of a cultural rejection of mainstream capitalist society; they want to be rebellious and cool. But the opposite is also true: some messengers were always anti-capitalist, and being a courier is the only job they can stomach. The vast majority, however, simply do the job and go home without worrying about style, appearance, or politics. The community of messengers is comprised of professionals, anarchists, activists, ne'er-do-wells, and many other cyclists who defy categorization.

Punk, the cultural theorists tell us, is a set of historical conjunctures that includes an amalgam of class-based resistance and hybridized style. In short it is a negation of mainstream culture. Bike messenger culture, with its hybrid stylistic expression represents a similar negation of mainstream car culture, though like punk it is shot through with contradiction. The messenger industry stands as a political expression of an alternative to fossil fuel consumption for many, yet to others it is just a job. Some clients hire messengers as a way to reduce their company's carbon footprint while to most it is just a cheap and efficient way to get things across town.

The allure of messengering for those in the punk rock community is clear: it is an outside job, free from the offices and the system of hierarchy and organization required by such jobs. The messenger can be a liminal *auslander* wandering the streets, both seen and unseen, in and out of the system, flying at lethal speeds, thriving on danger and loving the rush of human-powered vehicles and hating internal combustion engines. Like punk rock, a certain segment of the messenger community is minimalist, nihilist, and DIY. It is a community where you can be what you are and not be judged for it. Yet just like punk rock, it remains inside the system as well, and couriers do make judgments based on sex, race, and other superficial characteristics. The important difference between mainstream society and the punk and messenger communities is that such judgments are the subject of vibrant discussion.

Sex, Race, and Insecurity

Craig O'Hara writes that "there is no denying that sexism exists within the punk community," but goes on to say that it is not only discussed, but condemned, and this "is contrary to mainstream society where it is rarely condemned or even discussed by anyone other than feminists." The punk community's political ideology is at least in part based on "rejections of racism, classism, sexism and heterosexism" (O'Hara 1999: 103-4, 120). Both punk and messenger communities strive to be places were bigotry, homophobia, and sexism are not tolerated.

I sometimes jokingly refer to race, class, and gender as the holy trinity of sociology. These fractures of society have some influence on nearly everything we do. From the construction of our identity and our level of self-esteem to our life-chances and longevity, race, class, and gender have deep meaning and great effect. Though race or class or gender effects may not be reducible to rac*ism*, class*ism*, or sex*ism*, they are nonetheless important to note. 50 years after the dawn of the civil rights movements, African-Americans have a life expectancy 5.5 years shorter than an average American. Even 30 years after the second wave of feminism, women still earn 77 cents for every dollar a male earns. 25 years after Stonewall, same-sex couples still have no federal right to marry and experience discrimination by the government in branches like the military. Aside from these more passive forms of discrimination, there remain very active, pernicious, and violent forms. The homophobic murder of Mathew Shepard in Wyoming, the racist murder of James Byrd Jr. in Texas, or the "Jenna Six" episode in Louisiana are just a few examples. And even in communities where bigotry is thought to be minimal, it can rear its ugly head, such as the murder of the transgendered teenager Gwen Araujo in the Bay Area of California. Furthermore, unquestioned assumptions about race, class, sex, or heteronormalcy structure many of our thoughts and daily actions. Think of the person who cringes when a black man stands in line behind her at an ATM, or the police officer who stops a car on a pretext, because the car or the driver appears out of place for the neighborhood (NCIS 2002, US Census 2006, ACLU 1999).

Equality may be an ideal, but the reality of the messenger community includes sexism, racism, and other forms of prejudice. In many cities there are few non-white couriers and few women. One ten-year veteran, a woman who many look up to for her hard work, leadership, and skill, upon quitting as a courier had this to say:

> After about my 6th or 7th year the things that bugged me about the job were starting to crowd out the things that I loved about it. The number one thing that really made me start to hate the job was sexual harassment and sexual discrimination.

This particular courier has won many races, sometimes taking first as a female and first overall. Gender bias is a constant struggle though there are strong and skillful female couriers and there are woman-owned courier companies. Race organizers now strive to give equal prizes to male and female categories, but this was not always true. Overall, the racers in the profession are mostly young white men. Outside of racing, there are daily struggles with race and sex that many white male couriers are oblivious to.

That the most visible of messengers are predominantly white and male does not, *ipso facto*, make the community of messengers racist or sexist. But there are such elements. For example, though many couriers make it a point to be inclusive in language and action, labels are not always "politically correct." Many couriers ride brakeless track bikes and are both honored by those who admire the skill needed to ride one and vilified by those who believe that riding a bike without brakes at breakneck speeds in traffic is just plain dumb. A compromise position, to ride a fixed gear bicycle with brakes mounted in case of emergency, seems to get no respect from either side; such riders are branded a "bitch" or a "pussy."[7] To insult someone by using derogatory feminizing language is a clear expression of sexism.

Sexism thus comes from co-workers as well as clients and people on the street. One female courier in the US put it this way:

> Being a girl, and on top of that, being pretty small, I constantly have people telling me what I can't take. More often than not, I get the "Oh, I told them it was a box, I really don't think you can take it."

This messenger was discriminated against due to societal conventions and assumptions that male couriers will be able to carry larger or heavier loads. Of course the truth is a good distance from this assumption, as one male messenger noted in describing the difference between two co-workers: "the only woman working in our city as a messenger would routinely ride past [a male courier] carrying twice his load, at twice the speed." The only difference between men and women that could reasonably be argued has to do with upper body strength, and therefore the ability to heft a heavy bag onto the courier's back and onto the bike. And this difference is quite slight given the levels of physical ability demanded by the occupation: men and women both have to be physically quite fit to do the job well. This slight difference aside, once on the bike, there will be almost no difference in ability. The female courier went on:

> The same day I had a security guard tell me that he's 'old fashioned'—a nice way of saying sexist—and that it was disappointing to see a girl courier.

Her experience shows how sexism remains rampant in society, when someone in authority can cloak sexism under the label of "old fashioned" and proceed to insult a woman's ability. Of course societal sexism is only part of the problem, as this courier continued:

> And it's not just the clients. Though I do feel that my dispatchers are trying to be 'nice,' it makes me uncomfortable when they double check if the jobs are "something you can handle," I have never turned down an oversized bike job here and I have never heard them ask the boys that.

Dispatchers and co-workers make a set of assumptions about their female co-workers: that they are less able to carry big loads, that they might need more help, and that they might be slower or less able to aggressively navigate traffic. The urge to "double check" or an attempt to be "nice" is a politically correct way of expressing a sexist attitude; it is a sort of "sexism lite" based on biological assumptions. Many couriers chimed in on this point, suggesting that since female couriers were significantly above average for women in general, "the 'average' woman bike messenger can kick a lot more ass than the 'average' man. And the fastest woman courier probably isn't that much slower than the fastest male courier . . . The point is that biology can never justify sexism." Another courier put it succinctly: "Making judgments on anyone's abilities due to sex, stature etc. is bullshit . . . these 'noble' gestures just promote these power imbalances."

Sexist language is often but a symbol of an underlying attitude. Examples of this abound, including a recent exchange on a messenger email discussion list. A courier wrote about a scenario where a secretary crowed to him about buying a new SUV. He asked those on the discussion list how they would have responded, given couriers' general anti-SUV and pro-environment position, while recognizing that this secretary was the one responsible for making the call to the delivery company, and as such the courier had to be polite. Many people suggested various humorous come backs, but one male messenger responded by saying:

> Or, I suppose you could always humiliate her by grabbing her by the
> hair, straddling her [. . .] whilst shouting "How d'ya like my pimp
> cane, biyatch!" ;))))

The outrage from many couriers was strong and indignant. The writer offered up his apologies, but for some female messengers this was the last straw. What this type of comment shows is that there is a great deal of sexism in the messenger community, just as there is in the larger culture. Many messengers think that making crude and inappropriate jokes about rape is never tolerable, but just as clearly, the courier who said this thought that such jokes were acceptable.

Much of the overt sexism is self-policed, self-censored, or outright condemned when it is exhibited. But there is also a good deal of underground sexism. The messenger industry, as well as messenger culture, is a broadly male phenomenon. When female messengers show up to community events they attract a great deal of attention, in part due to their low numbers relative to men, and also for the simple fact that they are females who ride bikes, and male couriers might be understandably interested. But this attention is not necessarily invited or approved. Female messengers also have to deal with unwanted advances from dispatchers and clients, as the earlier quote suggests. The simple fact is that these women have to struggle with sexism on the job from supervisors, from clients, and from their male peers.

In addition to these on-the-job difficulties, there is a broad problem of gender dynamics in the messenger community. Much of messenger culture is centered on the development of skill in response to risk and danger, and this is often a typically masculine response focused on speed, agility, and old-fashioned daring-do. The job of messengering, one courier said,

> allows for a lot of male posturing in a lot of ways—who's got the baddest bike, who's the fastest, who's gotten into it with the most cars/peds/cops, trash talk about receptionists, depersonalized anger at suits/cube-dwellers/security guards, etc.

That there might be more subtle, less aggressive responses to negotiating traffic is either not noticed or not honored. There is a difficult navigation to make here, since many female riders successfully compete with males on the job and on the racecourse, so there are no foregone conclusions to be made about physical ability, the embrace of risky or aggressive behaviors, or other typically masculine responses to danger. But many male couriers think of their job and their culture as a largely male realm, with a few worthy females who can rise to their masculine level. This way of thinking is heavily misguided, as evidenced by a period of time when I worked at a courier company that was owned by a woman, dispatched by a woman, and the majority of couriers employed were female. One particularly astute courier connected male dominance in the messenger industry to notions of risk and authenticity, and the need to test one's abilities:

> I thought the reason for this industry being so male dominated was because of the way it tests inherently macho insecurity, ie boys want to go prove themselves as men enter the riskiest jobs they can find, usually the military, but if you're not much for that kind of thing or have other options, being a bike messenger is of course much more sexy. Throw in a little socioeconomic guilt and it's not hard to understand why this particular service industry is also pale and well-educated.

As this courier notes, like gender, race is similarly problematic. As an industry, bike messengering is not as "pale" as it is "male," but rather the most visible of the flashy messengers are "pale" and well-educated. Like women, couriers of color have a host of issues to contend with, from the subtle cues of co-workers to the broader patterns of racism in the larger society. Though most couriers were reluctant to talk about the difficult subject of race,[8] it is difficult to imagine that black couriers have as easy a time navigating building security as their white counterparts. And while it is true that some cities have strong minority representation in the courier industry, this has mostly to do with the socio-economic position of the occupation. Messengering is a dangerous, dirty, low-paying job. It is often the poor and under-educated from communities of color who fill the ranks of such risky jobs, and messengering is not different. The fact that it has become a cool job that can "test inherently macho insecurity" in an alienating world does not make it any less dirty or dangerous. All it means is that young white males on fixed gear bikes now compete with the many minority working class couriers for a slice of the meager pie.

Just as with the larger society, efforts to break away from sexist language and behaviors founders on the rocks of hierarchy, power, and inertia. As one courier said,

> This community without the women would be very dull and drab. These women are strong, powerful, smart, and generally witty. They bring a lot of color and insight into the community and god help us if we were to suddenly be without them. They go out there and work as hard as we do, then they kick our asses in races.

This messenger recognizes the value of women in the bike courier community, and honors their ability on the job and in community events like races. Overall, the subject of sexism is one that remains on the table, while the topic of race remains absent from discussion and obscured by the structure of the occupation.

BikePunk Culture

Bike messengers, then, are inside and outside the system at the same time. They both enable and reproduce the smooth functioning of capitalism and representative governance and yet many of them simultaneously embrace the anti-establishmentarian notions of punk. This cultural liminality—betwixt and between established categories—is expressed in the style endemic to the messenger scene. Like Hebdige's description of the punk subculture emphasizing hybridity and bricolage, the messenger look is pieced together based on style, efficiency, comfort, and utility. But this style, just as with punk, has come to be the hip urban cultural trend of the moment. As Nietzsche suggested in *The Gay Science*: "One thing is needful. 'Giving style' to one's character—that is a great and rare art!" Some of the more colorfully eccentric couriers found a way to "give style" to their character, and in many ways this has diffused through the community more broadly. Messenger style may not be a great and rare art, but the distinctive look has become a symbol of the accelerated life of the urban core, and has been taken up by those who admire this great and rare art of the couriers' style.

Jeff Kidder (2005) has argued that messenger style cannot be separated from action, the everyday working reality of messengering. While this is certainly true, one must look at the broad context of messengering in all of its forms. Kidder bases his ethnography on "lifestyle messengers" who live the style both on and off the job. He estimates this is perhaps 15 percent of the messengers in New York City, his site of research.[9] But if 15 percent of messengers act in a way that puts a high premium on a particular style, what does this tell us about the other 85 percent?   We can classify cyclists and style into four categories, as shown in the table below. Cyclists can be divided into those who have or have not worked as messengers, and those who do or do not display messenger style. Thus, cyclists who are not messengers and do not display messenger style can be called "commuters" or "sport cyclists" while those who do embrace messenger culture, but are not messengers, are labeled "posengers" or "fakengers."   In this formulation, "lifestyle" messengers who embrace messenger style and participate in messenger culture can be differentiated from "working messengers" who hang up their bikes at the end of the day.

Table 1. Messenger Style by Social Group

	Messenger Style	**No Messenger Style**
Messengers	Lifestyle Messengers	Working Messengers
Non-messenger Cyclists	"Fakengers" or "Posengers"	Commuters or Sport Cyclists

Many messengers dress distinctively, but avoid the sport cyclist's skintight lycra outfit and the commuter's highly visible fluorescent jersey. Though some messengers certainly do wear such clothes, most others would not be caught dead in them. Instead, messenger style includes baggy long shorts, or pants with one leg rolled up to clear the moving chain. These pants, shorts, or cut-offs often have many pockets to corral the various gear required by a messenger's day: pens, paper, manifest booklet, and a tough U-lock to defend against bike thieves (sometimes, instead of a U-lock a burly chain is worn over the shoulder or around the waist). Up top, messenger style includes a variety of shirts, but almost never the traditional lycra cycling jersey that racers wear (an exception is sometimes made for vintage wool cycling jerseys which have their own cultural caché). The standard skin-tight padded shorts of sport-cyclists are sometimes worn underneath the other gear. This helps eliminate chaffing but the shorts lack pockets, so utility shorts are worn on top. This functionality obscures the fact that there are many messengers who do not wear sport cycling clothes on the outside for fear of seeming unhip.

Some messengers use cycling shoes and clipped-pedal technology that fixes the foot to the pedals. This is terrifically efficient when on the bike but it makes walking through an office building difficult and slow. Many messengers instead employ standard platform pedals with "toe clips" or cages that strap the foot to the pedal, used with any normal sneaker or boot. Many messengers do not wear helmets, though this is quite variable by city and by messenger firm, as discussed in Chapter 3.

And what sort of bike does a flashy messenger ride? Increasingly over the last 20 years the answer has been a minimalist fixed-gear bicycle.[10] This is pure simplicity, with the additional advantage that nothing complex can bust in the middle of a day's work. They are cheap, durable, and easy to work on, hence they are "DIY." Many messengers leave the cushioned tape off their handlebars, giving them another distinctive look. As one messenger told a reporter, "I ride a fixed for money. For money only, because with a road bike you have to . . . after it rains, you have like two weeks of rain you have to replace your brake pads. After a month or two or riding hard on your gears you have to replace the cassette. And a track bike, its just bare bones bicycle" (Weyland 2007). This frugal and utilitarian perspective is closely aligned with messenger style.

The quality of urban hipness that messengers represent has been broadly co-opted by youngsters who want to cash in on messenger-chic. Every major city has its hip neighborhoods that recently began to fill up with youngsters riding fixies, carrying a courier bag, sporting messenger-style clothes. These posengers are faking a bike messenger pose, co-opting the style. And yet it is more complex than simple co-optation, since bike commuters, art school students, or other fakengers can be seen as simply learning the lessons that messengers have learned about durability, simplicity, and efficiency. While this is no doubt true in some cases, it does not fully explain the adoption of the many cultural markers of the messenger scene: the spoke cards from Alley Cat races, the patches and stickers on the messenger bag, the lack of handle bar tape, riding without a helmet, etc.

Who are these fakengers, and why do they mimic messengers? Messengers harbor many theories about who fakengers are, but the consensus is that they are young, urban hipsters. They might work in many professions, but most messengers think of them as art school students or graphic designers. In talking to a reporter, one messenger noted that "There might be a shift away from the culture being dominated by messengers to it being more dominated by . . . I dunno . . . computer guys . . . graphic designers" (Weyland 2007). In actuality, fakengers are merely early adopters in a trendsetting process. Many of them are, in fact, graphic designers, as well as web designers ("computer guys"), advertising and marketing workers, music promoters, students, and many others. Many of these trendsetters operate out of converted warehouses in the industrial part of town, have liberal work environments, and fit nicely into David Brooks' Bourgeois Bohemian category (Brooks 2000). The early adopters likely were exposed to messengers as part of their own jobs when they needed to send something across town by courier, and they can easily afford a new track bike that is beyond the price range of most working messengers.

So while there may be some antipathy towards the posenger, there is a synergy here, where the messengers also benefit from the expertise of the trendsetters. In one example, a courier company's client put together an edgy promotional campaign with pictures of the couriers next to off-beat advertising text, such as "Some of our couriers shave their legs for speed. Others are just plain kinky." Or "Gladly risking our necks for your stupid package."

Co-optation is never a simple process, as we have seen with the punk subculture—in some ways the Sex Pistols were an elaborate marketing ploy as evidenced by their final (and second) album, entitled "the great rock n' roll swindle." Just as hybridized punk clothes popularized by Johnny Rotten in 1977 can now be purchased at your local mall, track bikes and messenger gear can be found in many urban bike shops. The style that messengers developed by hybridizing cycling comfort and efficiency is now de-linked from those material realities and re-attached to symbolize urban coolness as a form of cultural capital that substitutes for real, monetary capital.

Messengers have a complex relationship to this process of co-optation. On one hand, the explosive growth of fixed gear bikes means that the frames and spare parts are cheaper and more widely available, including at specialty stores in some cities that focus entirely on fixed gear bikes. In fact, this phenomenon is so pervasive that even the New York *Times* has written on the topic, with an accompanying Internet photo and audio slide show (Weyland 2007). One NYC messenger on a delivery recently saw a fixed gear bike offered for sale in a posh clothing boutique. The bike was outfitted by a fashion designer, and was on sale for $6,000 (Whitesnake 2007).[11]

This process is not, of course, without its critics. Many messengers feel a sense of ownership about the messenger style, and derisively dismiss fakengers. In response to Whitesnake's online article cited above, one commentator posted on the website suggesting that the fashion designer should "go back to drawing lame-ass monkey faces" and went on to suggest that the bike was marketed to "hipsters who'll craigslist it for $500 in 2010."[12] Another courier told me "When people see us working and decide to make our jobs into a hobby or an image, of course we are going to think they're ridiculous. When people work so hard and spend a lot of money to look like messengers, we think it's even more ridiculous." One example of this is a rider by the name of Mayonnaise. In his self-published pamphlet called "Riding Fixed," Mayonnaise writes about dressing in cut off work pants and pushing a fixed gear around Chicago, showing up sport cyclists on $3,000 bikes, laughing at their amazement. To a messenger, this kind of posturing—including writing about it in a self-congratulatory style—would earn Mayonnaise the derogatory term of posenger.

Why do messengers dislike posengers? Aside from feeling ownership of the style, messengers might rationally fear for their jobs. As discussed earlier, posengers represent a "reserve army of labor" that might easily step in to take a messenger's job. If they are willing to go so far as to mimic messenger style, why would they not pick up a shift here and there, or take a break from their upscale job and "slum it" for awhile? Fakengers represent a vague threat to couriers' (already slight) job security, though couriers would never admit it. From their point of view, fakengers have no idea what they are doing, and wouldn't last two hours if they were actually put to the test (a view that is generally validated by Alley Cat races).

In large cities, such as New York with 3000 working couriers, many messengers are relatively unknown to each other, and so posengers may get by with anonymity. In smaller cities, most messengers know each other, or at least recognize each other. In a smaller community, social distance is more abbreviated. Messengers know each other, interact daily, and the in-group is more clearly defined. But with the proliferation of posengers it becomes harder to tell who is a lifestyle messenger and who is a fakenger in a hurry to get to the café. As social distance increases, solidarity wanes. With the introduction of uncertainty comes an atmosphere of distrust.

So posengers want to look like lifestyle messengers. Why do the lifestyle messengers dress and act distinctively? They are engaged in a form of capital substitution. Because of the low pay and high stakes of the messenger job, many messengers engage in cultural rent-seeking behavior: "if I can't get a living wage, at least I'll look cool while I'm at it." That is to say, since they are not earning monetary capital, they substitute by collecting cultural capital. These lifestyle messengers have become the latest icon of urban coolness, but no doubt the attention that comes with fad and fashion will wane in time.

What about the other 85 percent? Sadly there is not much to say that is as exciting and flashy as messenger chic. They ride in jeans, a t-shirt, and sneakers. They use a clunky old mountain bike purchased from the thrift store. In the rain they wear a poncho. They use a length of chain to secure their bike to the lamppost. No expensive U-locks, no special clothes, no special bikes. As one messenger put it:

> The most experienced people I met . . . were the ones that had crappy
> beat up old mountain bikes or three speeds and never seemed to be
> going any faster than 17 mph.

The bike might go home with them, or it might stay in the shop overnight. These messengers do not participate in the group activities described in the next chapter, and seemingly either reject messenger culture broadly or just simply can't be bothered as they have kids, non-messenger friends, or a non-bike related life. They, apparently, do not exhibit the need to offset low pay with cultural caché. But many others do, both messengers and non-messengers. They dress distinctively, ride recklessly, and don't wear helmets. They gather together and ride in packs, blowing red lights and stop signs, even off the job and on weekends. Why is it that messengers take the risk of flouting traffic laws without a helmet, even when they are off the job, and how does this relate to the structure of the occupation?

We can think of messengers as similar to Nietzsche's tightrope walker. In *Thus Spake Zarathustra*, Nietzsche's *ubermensch* encounters a crowd watching a tightrope walker. In the end the tightrope walker falls to his death. Rather than criticizing him, the crowd honors the tightrope walker for his bravery (Nietzsche 1978 [1885]). In some ways, "lifestyle" messengers are honoring the risk involved in the occupation by valorizing it. As discussed in Chapters 2 and 3, the structure of the occupation demands that messengers engage in risky behavior. This necessity of the job is then transformed into a cultural endeavor, where that risk is honored, like the brave tightrope walker. Messenger culture, then, valorizes what the occupation demands. Lifestyle messengers embrace risk even in their off-work lives as a way of expressing their belonging to a larger messenger community, differentiating themselves from mainstream society. Riding recklessly proves their belonging to a community and validates their bravery.

Conclusion

Messengers occupy a liminal position in our society. They are neither drivers, nor pedestrians—they are somewhere in between. This liminality underscores several challenges that messengers pose to sociology. They destabilize the bifurcation of work and play, and thus frustrate an easy analysis of alienation. They reproduce some racist and sexist dynamics, but tend towards tolerance and attempt to dismantle hierarchies in their communities. Some messengers adopt a punk and DIY attitude, but most of them just ride the streets, day-in and day-out.

Fakengers seek to mimic lifestyle messenger style and pose. Of course they are not mimicking the average working messenger on a beat-up bike, schlepping packages around town, suffering the indignities of racism and sexism. No, they mimic the young, white, male riders with the distinctive bike and flashy gear. What is it about this subculture that is so alluring to many young men in the hip neighborhoods of US cities, and why are they willing to spend so much money in the process? Simply put, messengers are cool. Their liminality—being both visible and invisible—gives them a certain cultural caché. In addition, the messenger style is a hybridized subcultural expression, similar to and overlapping with punk rock and anarchism. In this way it represents rebellion, an outside job free from business norms. It is culturally provocative. Posengers are cashing in on the same cultural capital that lifestyle messengers are, and often members of these two groups are superficially indistinguishable. But the difference is risk: lifestyle messengers are valorizing the risk required by the occupation, while fakengers are not undertaking those risks in the same ways and to the same extent. The graphic designer who floats an intersection while riding his fixie to his converted warehouse loft is making a choice to engage in risky behavior. But he is clearly not risking his neck for 8 hours a day. There is a community that forms around this exposure to danger, one where solidarity is maintained in the face of co-optation, but where selling out is another form of omni-present risk.

Notes

1. Quoted from a messenger posting a comment in an online discussion.

2. I acknowledge that I am using liminality as a metaphor, in some ways abstracting from Turner's work. The concept of liminality, however, has been used apart from the specific processes of rites of passage, transitional states of life, and pilgrimage that Turner originally studied (Bettis 1996; Errington 1990; King 1997). As Turner himself argued, the idea of liminality, when applied to complex modern societies, must be used as a metaphor (Turner 1982: 30).

3. The term subculture is contested and could imply that the stylistic content or identity is somehow less worthy than mainstream culture. I do not intend or condone such interpretations.

4. Greil Marcus (1990) and others argue that Malcolm McLaren was essentially looking for a way to sell more clothes from his London shop when he discovered Johnny Rotten and created the Sex Pistols. Using a style that combined the attire, attitude, and approach of Richard Hell, Iggy Pop, and the New York Dolls, the Sex Pistols were named after Malcolm MacLaren and Vivienne Westwood's London boutique SEX.

5. "Chain smokers" is a pseudonym.

6. A "mosh pit," or simply "a pit," is the term for an anarchic place on the dance floor at a punk rock concert where participants throw, slam, and hit one another. The term probably comes from the word mash, as in to mash potatoes. One, possibly apocryphal, story is that the ability to control someone by pulling their hair impelled punks to shave their heads, thus the popular skinhead look. Slamming into one another in a mosh pit (hence the label "slam dancing") may appear to an uninitiated observer as violent and chaotic but in fact, there are complex self-organized and self-enforced rules of behavior..

7. There is continual discussion among messengers at informal meetings, at races and gatherings, and in an online discussion forum about the "brakes or no brakes" issue. This possibly never-ending debate often takes the form of masculine posturing, hierarchy-asserting claims about skill, and contestation over what is rational or legitimate.

8. It is interesting that white male couriers were willing and enthusiastic in talking about sexism (especially in defining themselves as non-sexist), but a similar dynamic was not present in discussions about race. In fact, one messenger emphatically made the point that New York City has a large number of black couriers, and this somehow gave the imprimatur of post-racism to the entire community.

9. This estimate is probably high, with many more messengers hanging up their bikes at the end of the day and not caring much about the messenger "scene." This is indicated by the small turnout of NYC messengers at the world championships held in that city in 2005, where only a few hundred (perhaps 10 percent) of some 3000 NYC messengers showed up to the events.

10. A track bike, also known as a fixed-gear bike, or a "fixie," is a bicycle stripped

down to its most basic and historic elements. The bike has a single gear with no free-wheel, without a rear gear cluster, no front or rear derailleur, and often no brakes. The front ring and rear cog are connected via a highly tensioned chain, thus, when pedaled forward the bike will go forward, if pedaled backwards, the bike will go backwards. Those who ride without brakes apply reverse pressure on the pedals to slow down, or stand on the pedals to halt the rear wheel completely and skid to a stop. The reasons for riding such a contraption are myriad, and one is certainly style. But the bikes are also very light and thus very fast. They are cheap and durable under the pounding conditions of the messenger's day. This type of bicycle was developed for racing in a velodrome, a special bicycle-racing track, hence the name "track bike."

11. The average bike that "working" messengers ride might cost only a few hundred dollars, as would a fixed gear bike assembled from used parts. An average fixed gear "lifestyle" messenger bike, sold new, could cost $1,000. Sport bikes with full gears and made for road racing can easily cost $3,000 or more. Thus, a $6,000 fixed gear bike would never be confused with something that an average messenger might ride.

12. Craigslist (www.craigslist.com) is a popular Internet community and online marketplace of used products through free "classified" advertisements.

5. Bicycle Culture, Messenger Solidarity, and Community Matters

"There wasn't anything messengers couldn't do. We had our own races. We had our own 'zine. We even had our own bar and restaurant."

The risky and emotion-laden character of the bike messenger business, combined with its low pay, lack of benefits, and marginalized position forces messengers to find non-monetary remuneration in other realms such as cultural caché, but especially through community participation. Messengers maintain group cohesion through many activities, both formal and informal. They may meet at a normal gathering point during the lunch hour or at a local bar after work. They might participate in races on the local, regional, and global levels. They may participate in the local Critical Mass ride. And some simply hang up their bikes Friday at 5pm and don't look at them again until Monday morning. Group cohesion, like many things messenger, represents a baffling diversity; and yet many messengers manage to maintain a broad collective cohesion in the face of fragmentation.

Messenger meetings I: The Local Alley Cat race

It was a cold and wet Saturday morning and we had to drive an hour to where the race was held. We rolled into the messenger shop at 7:30 for the 8AM race. The shop is not much more than an old warehouse with a cracked cement floor and beer cans and cigarette butts covering all available surfaces: tables, chairs, window ledges, and the floor. A few lockers lean precariously against one wall and there is an office in a corner with a disheveled desk, two phones, and an outdated computer. There is a vile-looking and worse-smelling bathroom containing more beer cans than toilet supplies. But mostly there are bikes and bike racks everywhere. Chaos rules: there is no rhyme or reason. The bikes are jammed into the racks that are crowded into the shop that is shoehorned between buildings at the end of an alley. But it is downtown and the rent is cheap. Such is the office of a local courier company that is putting on the "Alley Cat" race. We signed in, paid the $10 entry fee, and joined the crowd comparing bikes and swapping stories while several messengers had a foamy breakfast of Miller Genuine Draft.

A crowd formed around the tricksters as they showed off in the alley outside. They did their stuff—having fun and warming up. One guy performed no-handed skids on his fixed-gear track bike. Another rode his backwards in easy figure eights. A third stood up on the top tube of his bicycle, surfing the parking lot on his trusty steed. Then we mobilized for the start line a couple miles away in the industrial section south of the city, right on the water.

An Alley Cat is not formally called a "race" because it is an illegal, underground venture. Calling it a race implies sponsors, insurance, and prizes—none of which are generally involved. Modest entry fees are collected, pooled, and given to the high finishers—the money usually ends up buying beer for all the participants at the end of the race. The race itself can take many different forms, but all mimic the trials of a messenger's workday. The most basic is a list of delivery addresses made up by the organizers that the riders must visit (sometimes in a specific order, other times not). In some races the rider may have to perform a feat (popular examples include doing push ups or hopping over barricades while carrying the bicycle). The winner is the first rider to complete all of the tasks and visit all of the addresses.

The race offers a time and place for messengers to gather and recreate their community through good-natured competition. They may have many differences, but all have one thing in common: cycling in the city. Some may drink, smoke, and ride like lunatics. Some have given up substance use, but still ride like lunatics. Others are straight-edge professionals in training for spring races. Still others are simply trying to make ends meet. Alley Cats are a place to produce and reproduce their solidarity with one another, as well as their antipathy towards autos. During an Alley Cat race, with 20 or 30 cyclists in a group, cars lose their normal advantage and cyclists can dominate the road. By taking over the streets and engaging in playful yet competitive forms of solidarity, messengers in Alley Cat races reaffirm their status as members of their peculiar community.

In this race, after a map was passed around with the delivery locations listed on it, someone at the head of the group of 20 cyclists dropped a U-lock to simulate a starting gun and we were off. We ran to get our bikes from where they were all leaning against a fence, but the first messenger to his bike managed to knock down the rest. He sprang into the lead while everyone else extracted their bikes from the tangled pile. We commenced chasing him down. The track riders are often the fastest, and sure enough after a four block all-out sprint that separated the field of racers, I found myself with two others trailing the first place rider, who lead us by a city block. Since I had no knowledge of the city, I introduced myself to the two racers next to me. One was from a city farther north, and the other was, happily, a local. I suggested that we could compete against one another and all lose, or we could work together and try to catch the leader. The local could tell us where to go, and all three of us would co-operate on pulling.[1]

We worked together but the other rider was almost immediately out of sight. He took a left where we took a right and we did the deliveries in a different order. At each stop we would see other racers doing the drops and moving on, all of them choosing their own routes through the city. We crossed cobblestone streets that in the wet morning weather made turns impossible, and riding in a straight line difficult. The city is built at the meeting place of two rivers, and the racecourse crossed multiple metal bridges known by local messengers as "cheese graters." They get extremely slick when wet, and if you fall down on them, they'll gouge out your flesh as if you were made of soft cheese. Luckily, no one did that day.

After riding through 12 deliveries in about 45 minutes and covering 20 miles worth of city streets, we finally came to the last address, listed on my manifest sheet simply as "the garage." Not knowing anything about it, I followed the local racer around a wet turn when he suddenly took off in an all-out sprint. Our companion had tired long ago and lagged behind, so it came down to me and the local guy. He raced, I raced, and we came down the street next to each other at breakneck speeds—easily 30 miles per hour. All of my focus was on the sprint: making sure not to hit the rider 6 inches to my left, avoiding a rain-slickened manhole cover, jumping around an opening car door, when all of a sudden I caught the flash of a sign in the corner of my eye: blue neon advertised a local bar called The Garage. I was between the other rider and the parked cars when my companion headed toward a curb cut outside the bar—I did the same, half to avoid him and half to beat him to the finish. We both went into a skid but he stopped more quickly than I and we went down, grinding to a halt on the sidewalk in a jumbled mess. Jumping up, we presented our manifest sheets to the race official at the same moment and were proclaimed a tie . . . for second place. The other local who took off a block in front of us at the start of the race beat us by about a minute.

We proceeded into the bar where the race organizers had already launched into a round of beers. We congratulated them on a great race-course, and swapped stories of "skitching" rides[2] around the city and trying not to go down on the cobblestones, comparing wounds. The prizes were awarded: $60 for first place male and female, $30 each for second, and prizes for furthest traveled/highest-placed, and most blood. DFL (Dead Fucking Last) was awarded a special trophy. The happy congregation proceeded to revel in the collective effervescence of a modern moment of mechanical solidarity. Instead of plying their trade all over the city, going different directions, servicing different clients, and perhaps in competition for deliveries, the Alley Cat race is a time when messengers can come together to focus on their similarities, to exercise their solidarity, and to engage in friendly competition for bragging rights.

What is common to this process of socialization is the odd amalgam of anarchistic rejection of authority combined with hierarchical competition. The outgrowth of this is DFL, which seems to suggest that if prizes have to be offered to structure the community, then perhaps one of those categories should be for last place. In an Alley Cat the overall winner sometimes gets a prize of equal value as the overall loser. This winning-by-losing category of DFL is similar to "shooting the moon" in the trump-game "Hearts." It takes a certain amount of calculation to manage to finish within a prescribed time frame and come in exactly last. Thus, the DFL is not the least experienced, nor the worst messenger. He or she is, however, often the most gregarious and fun-loving of the racers.

Not all Alley Cats are like this, but all are serious on some level. Most are smallish affairs and draw only from local crowds. Others are more regional, inviting messengers from nearby cities to compete for a plane ticket to the national or global championships. One Alley Cat is famed for its serious attempt at a lack of seriousness. It is held in late

January in Minneapolis, Minnesota. It can be 30 degrees below zero, often with plenty of snow and ice. As if that wasn't enough, each stop requires the rider to drink a different form of alcohol—checkpoints are often bars. Since it is always run on the same day as the famous football game, they call it The Stuporbowl.

Messenger meetings II: National and global gatherings

In addition to uncountable local and regional races, there are continental championships such as the European Cycle Messenger Championships (ECMC) and the North American Cycle Courier Championships (NACCC) that attract hundreds of racers, and a global competition with thousands of messengers, the Cycle Messenger World Championships (CMWC). True to the humble focus on fun and community, in such competitions the victor wins little more than a new messenger bag and bragging rights for the next year. The national, regional, and global races are different from Alley Cat races: they are structured, sanctioned, legitimate events. They draw anywhere from several hundred to several thousand riders and thus must involve a closed-course and carry insurance. For these reasons, the event is altered from the all-out, no-holds-barred improvisation of an Alley Cat, and there is usually no DFL category. The large events do, however, serve their own solidarity function for the larger messenger community.

In December of 2002 I attended the North American Cycle Courier Championships (NACCC) in Houston, Texas. Such a race is a massive undertaking: Where a local Alley Cat may draw 20 or even 50 riders, the championship races often draw several times this number from all over the region, and beyond. The event in Houston was a three-day party, with lots of beer, lots of riding, and lots of live music—generally punk rock. One courier from Ireland told me that in the Cycle Messenger World Championships (CMWC) and the NACCC "the final C should really stand for Celebration." In fact, there are only modest rules governing the race, one of which is that riders must be "at least mildly sober."

Such national and continental races offer a place for traveling messengers to meet up with one another and celebrate their friendship and their chosen profession. I saw colleagues who had moved on to different cities fly off their bikes to greet one another. Even though technically a continental gathering the races draw messengers from all over the world. At the North American race there were participants from Germany,

Ireland, and the Netherlands as well as Canada and the US.[3] Reminiscent of Grateful Dead fans selling trinkets in the parking lots of concerts, one courier from Berlin was selling t-shirts to finance his trip.

This motley crew sat around in the sun in the warehouse district in Houston, watching and participating in the qualifying rounds of the race. The racecourse threaded around the warehouses, across railroad tracks, over potholes and amongst the strewn detritus of an industrial city. The organizers had developed the course location with the approval of city officials, the police were notified that a special event was occurring, and the course itself was closed to automobile traffic due to insurance requirements. 50 riders per group went through five heats of one-hour qualifying races, with the fastest overall riders making it into the final race the next day. Those waiting to race or those just finishing wandered around talking, drinking, carousing, swapping cycling caps, stenciled t-shirts, and comparing the relative virtues of various messenger bags. Tricksters played at track-stands and performed backwards figure-8s on their bikes. As discussed in Chapter 4, the Chain-smokers typify the bikepunk demeanor. Throughout the qualifying rounds they spray-painted, carved, and otherwise abused their bikes, all the while swilling cheap beer. As quoted earlier, after a dismal showing in the qualifying sessions one of them announced loudly "maybe we should go into rehab so we can win some races!" At one point, one of the less wild members wandered up to my companions and asked for a drink of water. "Don't tell the guys," he said softly, "they don't like it when we drink anything other than beer."

The carnival atmosphere extended into the evening's festivities, centered on a live music show of three local punk bands in one of the warehouses. Outside, people milled around a sizable bonfire, drinking beer and eating signature Texas barbeque. A mechanical bull was set up in one side of the yard, far away from the bonfire, and messenger after messenger tried their luck at riding a different mount. The couriers partied late into the night, heedless of the main race the next morning. Well after midnight, when things got frenzied, couriers began to jump through the flames across the bonfire pit.

Given the revelry of the night before, it was predictable that the 9AM start time of the main race was pushed back to after 11. The race itself differed from the qualifying heats. It was four hours long, with racers completing as many manifest sheets as possible. The racers rode their legs off for four hours straight, and those who did not qualify cheered on the contestants; occasionally tossing empty (and sometimes full) beer cans onto the racecourse. The top ten victors were announced soon after the race, and last night's party re-started.

Following the main race was a series of trickster events: the skid competition, the trackstand race, sprints, and the bunny hop. The skid and trackstand competitions involve only fixed gear bikes to show off the rider's skill. To stop a fixie with no brakes the rider most stop pedaling and "lock up" the rear wheel, thereby skidding to slow or stop. The competition involves riding as fast as possible towards a chosen mark on the pavement, and then locking up the rear wheel and skidding for as long a distance as possible. The winner, Chipmunk, skidded for more than 250 feet, or about the length of a city block, on smooth pavement.

The trackstand competition is also performed on fixed gear bikes, where the rider stays upright but perfectly still.[4] Riders rock slightly in place—generally there are delimited areas that the competitors cannot roll outside of. Whoever can hold this balanced position the longest will win the prize. As couriers got better and better at this over the years of racing, the competition had to be altered as some riders could literally sit in this position for hours. Now a trackstand competition goes for two minutes (more or less) after which riders must remove one hand from the handlebars. After a minute in this position, the second hand must be removed, leaving them sitting on their bikes, feet on the pedals, with their hands in the air. After another minute, any riders still upright must take one foot off the pedals. There are few people who can hold a one-footed trackstand for more than a few seconds, and this is the person who wins the motionless "race." After the trackstands, the same riders pedaled their fixies in backwards circles, with the prize again going to Chipmunk, who managed 13 full backwards circles.

In Houston the most stunning post-race competition was unintentionally saved until last: the bunny hop. Two low standards were set out, with a pole running between them like a high jump bar at a track-and-field event. Contestants rode up towards the bar and lifted their front wheel up into the air, pulling the rear wheel behind and over the bar. Rider after rider jumped and cleared, jumped and failed. The bar advanced from 12 inches to 14 to 16, and eventually to above two feet. All but a few riders had missed, knocking themselves out of the race. The final few jumped and jumped, taking the bar near to three feet high, which is about as high as most upright bicycles. Finally there were only two bunny hoppers left. At just an inch from three feet, both riders jumped and failed. They each took a second attempt and failed. Unhappy with the idea of co-winners, as dusk settled the crowd demanded a "bunny hop-off."

Instead of judging by height, the organizers decided to construct a run-off competition by length of jump. Three brave couriers lay shoulder to shoulder on the pavement, and in turn the two competitors rode madly towards their companions, and at the final moment launched themselves into the air and jumped over them. Another courier laid down in the line, and the two jumpers cleared them. A fifth courier laid down, and the more sensible (and less drunk) spectators tried to stop the madness. Undeterred, the racers jumped and made it. It was getting dark. One of the organizers placed some blinking bike lights at the front and back of the line of prone couriers (with a blinking red beacon, the jumpers could more adequately judge the distance). The racers jumped again, and again, eventually clearing ten messengers laid shoulder to shoulder, a distance of perhaps 20 linear feet. In the dead of night under dim streetlights, they finally declared the two jumpers co-winners of the bunny hop competition.

In July of 2005 I participated in the 13th annual Cycle Messenger World Championships (CMWC) in New York City. With thousands of messengers from all over the world, it was an astounding sight. The NY Bike Messenger Association office in SoHo housed the headquarters for the three-day event, with side-events happening in several of the boroughs of the City. The main racecourse was located across the river in Jersey City. Watching hundreds of couriers ride the PATH train under the Hudson River was just one of the oddities that New Yorkers were treated to that weekend.

The Jersey City financial district is broadly unoccupied on the weekends, so the racecourse could be closed to traffic except for one road open through the middle, monitored by uniformed police officers. Removed as it was from the heart of the City, the World Championships (or "worlds") could offer two important, if countervailing gifts to couriers. First, it offered a gathering place removed from tourist scrutiny and interference, and so more craziness could ensue. It was also marginalized from the energy and the hotspots of culture and entertainment of New York City. Riders were haphazardly lodged with friends (new and old) across several boroughs of the City, sometimes many miles from the race location.

The racecourse itself offered much in terms of entertainment. Revelry was ubiquitous, as in Houston, but with a stronger international flare. One Scottish courier rode in a homemade kilt. Japanese couriers brought special Keirin racing bikes.[5] And in preparation for their qualifying race, two topless, very drunk Dubliners ran afoul of the police directing traffic. The Dubliners were hammered drunk, barely able to pilot their trusty steeds while drinking extra-large cans of beer. The flummoxed cop who stopped them said, "There are so many laws you're breaking right now I don't know which one to arrest you for." Surrounded by so much iniquity, and so many couriers who were not about to let a cop ticket their fellows, he ended up letting them off with an exasperated warning: "Just finish your beers and go!"

Apart from the main race, which showcased the best 300 messengers riding their legs off, one highlight of the weekend after the race was when locals led a "Critical Mass" style group ride of some 1500 cyclists north through Hoboken, across the George Washington Bridge, and down the West Side Highway: about 20 miles at a moderate cycling pace, snarling traffic behind us for miles.

The Houston and New York City events represent a typical bike courier gathering. Messengers congregated to have fun, ride their bikes, and find out who was the fastest courier in North America or the world. Emile Durkheim relates a typical bifurcation of social processes in describing the "corroboree" ([1912] 1995: 217). On one side is the monotonous daily activity, on the other the momentous social gathering. Like the Aboriginal Australians that Durkheim studied, the day-to-day grind of a messenger's day stands in contrast to large race gatherings. "These two phases stand in the sharpest possible contrast," Durkheim noticed:

> The first phase in which economic activity predominates, is generally
> of relatively low intensity. Gathering seeds or plants necessary for
> food, hunting, and fishing are not occupations that can stir truly
> strong passions. The dispersed state in which the society finds itself
> makes life monotonous, slack, and humdrum.

But all of this changes when the ceremonial meeting known as the corroboree occurs:

> The very act of congregating is an exceptionally powerful stimulant.
> Once the individuals are gathered together, a sort of electricity is
> generated from their closeness and quickly launches them into an extraordinary height of exaltation.

At the big gatherings messengers experience something like the collective effervescence that Durkheim describes. Everyone is focused on the same events, on building relationships, on having fun. Though the spiritual aspect is absent at courier races, exaltation is at the core. And yet, as noted previously, messengers also challenge Durkheim's bifurcation of social processes. Forms of this collective energy that are so apparent in the races are also identifiable during the daily grind of a courier's day. When they hail each other, congregate at slow moments, or grin and slap a high-five as they pass in the street during a run, messengers are blurring the lines between work and play. They are emphasizing identity and in-group membership, and experiencing something analogous to collective effervescence.

The CMWC and the NACCC symbolize several processes of messenger group dynamics. First, such races are moments when the messenger identity is re-affirmed and re-inscribed for individuals within the profession. They meet up with friends from afar, joining in a ritual of solidarity and camaraderie.

Social events like these are also clear instances of Durkheimian collective effervescence. Durkheim argued that ritual gatherings, such as animist religious events, were moments when social groups came together and increased collective energy in an upwards spiral. These moments were significant due to their ability to bind members one to another, affirming their solidarity (Durkheim [1912] 1995: 379):

> The rites serve . . . to maintain the vitality of those beliefs and to prevent their memory from being obliterated—in other words to revitalize the most essential elements of the collective consciousness and conscience. Through this rite, the group periodically revitalizes the sense it has of itself and its unity; the nature of the individuals as social beings is strengthened at the same time.

The good-natured competition of races clearly serves this social function. Members are raised up by the energy flowing among the group. They push one another to new heights of achievement (and sometimes lunatic antics) through the collective vigor.

The rituals of these gatherings sometimes involve the transgression of socially imposed boundaries; binges of substance use, nudity, and daredevil bike stunts all serve to define those inside the group as opposed to outsiders. "Tourists" and "citizens" are tolerated as a friendly audience, but the feats are enacted primarily to demonstrate collective solidarity. On an individual level they also serve to cement one's identity as group member. The racing rituals thus function on the individual and group level to define inclusion, enforce solidarity, and re-inscribe identity.

Social rites often involve feats of strength, endurance, skill, and sometimes consciousness-changing chemicals. Yaqui Indians use peyote cactus to get closer to the spirit world, Pentecostal Christians use strychnine to demonstrate the power of faith. And so it is with messenger races: they are rituals of solidarity fueled by beer and punk rock, based on feats of skill and strength, performed in sociable competition for an audience of the in-group (and some out-group) members.

Cashing in/Selling out

Bike messengers can simultaneously have a strong commitment to their community and yet be fiercely individualistic. As in many loosely knit groups, there are very strong opinions in contradictory directions, and this is especially true on the subject of corporate sponsorship, the control of the messenger image, and the meaning of messenger identity. The derision toward posengers is an illustration of this, but it comes to its sharpest focus on the issue of selling out. In the lead-up to the 13th annual World Championships in New York in 2005 (CMWC XIII) there were fierce discussions about these issues, culminating a year later with a practical joke perpetrated on the global messenger community by a group calling themselves "Messenguerilla."

The NYC CMWC organizing team had a monumental set of challenges. They needed to manage as many as 3,000 messengers coming into town to events dispersed across most of the five boroughs. They had to secure spaces for events over three days and ensure security, all while managing the press, the police, and the local governments. They settled on locating the main race in New Jersey when the NYPD, due to terrorism concerns, balked at a large event that coincided with Independence Day weekend.

One challenge that the organizers struggled with was establishing a copyright to the name and symbols associated with the CMWC. In an effort to keep the name from being co-opted by a commercial group, they trademarked it, causing some consternation among other groups and individuals around the globe. They then proceeded to secure funding through sponsorship by several corporations, including companies that produce messenger merchandise. Messenger bag companies like Manhattan Portage, Timbuk2, and Chrome often sponsor races, so this was not out of the ordinary. As is the practice at many sponsored events, corporate logos figured prominently on t-shirts, the program of events, and other gear. In order to pay to insure the race, sponsor funding is a necessity. Participation by companies was relatively uncontroversial, especially since ex-messengers founded some of them.

What was more controversial was the inclusion of the athletic clothing manufacturer, Puma:

> I've heard a lot of on & under the surface grumbling/shit-talk about the CMWC's in NYC over the last year and Puma's involvement . . . I also know a bit of what it took to throw the CMWC's in NYC and it sucks that anyone would talk shit given all the time work energy commitment love heart and soul etc that went into throwing that event.

One courier went on to express dismay over where such corporate sponsorship might lead:

> I would really hate to see the cmwc turn into something like the x-games.

Another courier expressed an anti-corporate position, but recognized the reality of putting together such a grand undertaking:

> I would have loved to do CMWC without corporate sponsorship, and having done one Championship, I know what goes into putting it on and how exponentially that would be increased by doing it without corporate backing.

This member of the organizing team was responding to a low-level (but sometimes outright) concern expressed before and after the race. Many couriers balked at seeing Puma's name on water bottles (which the company provided for free), t-shirts (also free to all registrants), and the company's presence at the event itself. This courier justified the inclusion of the company based on impeccable logic:

> Does the community benefit from an event like that? Absolutely. It's high profile, gets media coverage (which lends to people taking messengers seriously when we're trying to get funds for things like the BMEF) and [. . .] it also gets respect for messengers on the street, and lending credence to the idea that messengers are worthwhile human beings, have very real skills, and are not the "lazy", "can't-get-a-real-job", "kids" that so many suits and other people take messengers to be.

But sadly that logic was faced with a somewhat heavy emotional response. Anti-corporate arguments were based on many of the positions discussed throughout this book: a generally left-leaning political stance, often times laced with anarchistic and anti-capitalist perspectives, along with a fear of co-optation and exploitation of the messenger image. Anti-corporate feelings were strongly, but calmly expressed by many:

> I think that it's the nature of corporations to use everything they can for marketing, to claim everything as their own by slapping a label/logo on it and using whatever culture is cool for the moment to push their own street cred to sell their product. It's called cultural taxidermy, where they rip the skin off of something meaningful and flip a soul-less version of it for profit.

This courier, clearly well-informed about corporate behavior, identifies exactly the set of interests that Puma has with sponsoring messenger events. As mentioned in the previous chapter, in the year before the CMWC, Puma went so far as to sponsor a team of messengers to race in official cycling events around the nation: Team Puma. Established through the organizational efforts of a long-time messenger and one of the lead organizers of the CMWC event in New York, Team Puma was envisioned as bringing together the fastest messengers from New York (self-described simply as the fastest messengers). Through a series of velodrome competitions, the winning messengers would join Team Puma and receive generous support for their racing:

> The top scoring messenger competitors will be picked to join Team
> PUMA . . . These riders will receive custom bikes and PUMA gear.
> Team PUMA will travel to other cities, racing and representing. Ho-
> tel and airfare included.

The custom track bikes and athletic gear are far beyond what most messengers could afford, and the organizer, Kevin "Squid" Bolger, argues that this is a way for messengers to finally get their due. As one messenger said: "we may as well grab our slice of the pie and at least have some active involvement in the way we're being spun." It is a way to make use of the urban cool that messengers represent. Since messengers are heavily exploited in the occupational realm, why not cash in on the cultural caché and gain cultural capital while letting the corporation buy you a new bike—who cares if the corporation's name is all over it?

Squid sees Team Puma as a legitimation strategy. In a New York *Times* article (Staff 2005) he said:

> We want people to think more of us than just that guy who ran over
> their foot . . . We also want to improve work conditions, since most
> messengers are underpaid and get no medical insurance.

Winning mainstream cycling races with Team Puma gives the imprimatur of the sporting world, helping to move the messenger image beyond "the 'lazy', 'can't-get-a-real-job', 'kids' that so many suits and other people take messengers to be" as the courier quoted above so succinctly put it. The visibility, Squid hopes, will allow for messengers to gain respect. The fact that they get some free gear along the way helps.

Team Puma members think of themselves as an elite group, and they certainly are. Winning a series of velodrome races qualifies them as some of the fastest messengers in New York, and Alfred Bobe, a team leader, was also the fastest fixed gear rider in the 2005 NACCC. In the same New York *Times* article, Bobe described the benefits that messengering brings to mainstream cycling events:

> Messengers have better instincts and reflexes, and a lot sharper peripheral vision. If you're not conscious and in the moment at all times, you can die on someone's car door. That's what separates us from regular racers. We have a different inner core and strength because our messenger work is our training.

Squid elaborated:

> There's a certain ability you get by messengering that you can't get from the road or the track . . . We ride wearing a 20-pound lock and a 40-pound bag. When you finally get to the track and take all that off, you feel explosive, like you have wings.

As discussed in the previous chapter, many messengers claim this elite status as part of the social psychology of everyday risk-taking. But Team Puma adds to this the layer of athletic competition.

While Squid argues that this is a way for messengers to cash in, others suggest that it is more like "selling out." Those who cried "sell out!" about CMWC sponsorship and Team Puma were attempting to keep their profession pure. Many commentators made reference to the trajectory of skateboarding and mountain biking, both of which had humble subcultural origins that were co-opted and exploited to become major mainstream corporate moneymakers. Messengering and messenger races, these couriers argued, had to remain free of such abuse.

Other couriers argued that the righteous stance against selling out meant denying access to cultural and financial capital for those who gained sponsorship. But one courier noticed that this gain for some racers was built on the exploitation of others:

> Face reality: Team Puma is buying street credibility. And a couple of messengers have fun racing while millions of people in their indian factorys are dying of tuberculosis. World is evil, Che Guevarra is dead and Muhammad Ali is batty. There's no more heroes.

The argument over cashing in versus selling out, however, was not played out only on the individual level. Since Squid was a major organizer of the CMWC, and corporations like Puma were involved, this led to all messengers participating in the event being branded by Puma's desire for "street cred" and "cultural taxidermy." In fact, the deepest irony came on the day of the race, when the Team Puma support vehicles showed up at the racecourse carrying the Team's bicycles. The official vehicle was a fully outfitted Hummer H2 and trailer, complete with Puma logo and specialized paint job. To many messengers, this vehicle represents everything that they stand against: excessive fossil fuel consumption, domination of the roads, the very real risk of death at the wheels of a massive SUV. In short, Hummers represent vehicular hubris.

Just when the furor over selling out to corporations had about died down, one year after the NYC world championships someone claiming the name of "Messenguerilla" sent an anonymous email to the international email discussion list:

> Beware Sellouts,
> You're only just starting to sell your souls and you're feeling nice, but the sunny days are counted. The underground is moving and will fight the evil corporate powers and you, their helping helpers.
> We are not willing to accept what is going on in the phony messenger race circus. The Messenguerilla, the movement of the free-minded messengers, is ready to strike back. You can count on us to be present at future CMC's.
> We shall not tolerate any bondage!
> We are not for sale!

The writer later sent two more missives to the list, reproduced in part below:

> We urge you, too, to reflect on your willingness to accept the grip of corporate powers on messenger events and to sharpen your senses pertaining to the unfriendly takeover of your values. . . . Traffic-free racecourses, electronic surveillance devices attached to every bike, police-escorted critical mass rides, commercialized messenger parties are only just the most obvious hazards. Others still need to be identified. Many more need to be addressed.
> The Messenguerilla is still holding up the fight for you and the entire messenger community. Together we stand up for our ideals. Everyone who cares about the future of the cycle courier culture should support the movement of The Messenguerilla. You should not take anonymity for weakness. We have choosen anonymity because it is not a battle of individuals it is the battle of a community, OUR COMMUNITY!

These open letters to the messenger community provoked a strong response from messengers the world over, especially in the US:

> I have refrained up to this point, in responding to your utter lack of decorum, respect and general intelligence when posting to this list. But this is the limit! YOU YELLOW RAT BASTARD COWARD. If you think your opinion is so valuable as to have to inform the world about it, then sign your friggin name. Do you think you can hide behind the web's anonymity, insult everyone and still have any credibility? Stand up for once in your sorry life and be accountable. Try posting something constructive or at the least helpful, intllegently provocative, insightful or humorous.

Aside from the concern over anonymity, many messengers were taken aback by the self-righteousness of the writer, the aggressive tone of the letters, and the rigid stance towards defending the inclusive community that no one owned. One messenger chided the Messenguerilla for criticizing from a position of naivité:

> ok, lets make this an official rule: if you haven't ever thrown a cham
> pionship-scale event, or tried to do something for somebody that re
> quires large sums of money (ie. sending riders to a foreign country,
> supporting a team with bicycles, etc.), DON'T TALK SHIT ABOUT
> HAVING CORPORATIONS INVOLVED.

But soon more reasoned replies came out through discussion. One courier succinctly asked "how can anybody be for selling out?" Others went more deeply into the challenge and response:

> the [Messenguerilla] made some outrageous remarks that obviously
> offended some people which is too bad, but i think some people are
> being way too thin-skinned and too paranoid. get a sense of humor al
> ready. just because they yelled "sellout" doesnt mean they were talk
> ing about "you". a bunch of people sure got real defensive real quick
> though, didnt they? personally i agree that the name calling is per
> haps a bit unnessesary, but i think it is just part of the act. i believe
> they were just saying a bunch of outrageous shit to get everyone's at
> tention and guess what, it worked.

This well-respected courier expressed the feelings of many on the international messenger email list, once the more emotional diatribes had died down. Messenguerilla clearly was taking a strong stance against sponsorship and corporate involvement. But it rapidly became clear to many that Messenguerilla was pulling an elaborate practical joke on the high-minded and sometimes self-righteous US messengers. Messenguerilla, it became clear, was a group of European messengers who subsequently participated in the European Cycle Messenger Championships (ECMC). One messenger from Spain told me that the entire exercise was a joke. Not many Americans laughed at it.

The Messenguerilla escapade did advance an interesting discussion about the nature and extent of corporate involvement in the messenger world:

> Just for the record I see corporation's as "useful tools" with the word
> "tools" having a double meaning. While we're all fashionable in an
> urban- cowboy sort of way. I say we should take advantage of it. To a
> point. Where that point is, each of us has to figure out for ourselves.

The recognition of messengers as representing urban cool is again used as a justification for cashing in on cultural capital. But the more nuanced point is crucial here: everyone has got to figure out for themselves what they are comfortable with. Forcing all messengers to participate in a Puma-sponsored CMWC violates the principle of individualism expressed by the courier above. But another messenger acknowledged it obliquely, handily summing up the punk rock/DIY attitude of many messengers:

> the idea is that we, as a community are who make up our champion-
> ships, and that we all have the ability to make our community and
> events better, without corporate sponsorship. we can do it ourselves.

Still other messengers saw the deep irony in trying to remain pure in the face of co-optation and corporate involvement. One messenger called out his colleagues on the contradiction:

> I suggest you first get your company to dump all of its evil corporate
> clients, for whom you really work, and start delivering only for lo-
> cally run small business, before lambasting those who are working in
> an arena that could actually allow us to benefit in some way from the
> eventual and inescapable co-opting of the messenger image, which
> has been proceeding since long before most of us on this list ever
> started work on the streets

This messenger details the unavoidable contradiction between the daily reproduction of capitalism and wanting to keep corporations at bay during special events. He also questions the legitimacy of some potentially neophyte commentators.

Finally, after letting the pot boil merrily away for several weeks, Messenguerilla wrote to the list again to clarify the position:

> I'm a messenger that is trying to keep courier-events real, free of
> huge mega sponsorshit, and with a little bit more fun.

In summing up the Messenguerilla position, it became clear that the whole provocative charade was meant to make a point about the ability of corporations to corrode the messenger community. Another well-respected messenger replied:

> That's why I like having the messenguerilla around. It keeps the dis-
> cussion about the role of corporate sponsorshit (I frickin' love that
> term) on the table. . . . I'm sorry, but while people are getting ex-
> ploited at this job, I really can't get too teary about the "selling out"
> of our image. So some corporate fucks are making money off of our im-
> age—Newsflash, messengers are urban "cool" and corporate fucks
> are pros at making money off the flavor of the minute.

While no one is really in favor of selling out, many couriers are intensely suspicious of corporate involvement in their community, and act strenuously against co-optation. The DIY spirit of the messenger community makes it difficult for the juggernaut of capitalism to make full use of the messenger image, try as they might. As one courier told me in 2002: "This is the only non co-opted, dynamic, vibrant punk rock subculture left. They tried to co-opt it but we fuckin' resisted." Even mighty resistance against the capitalist juggernaut eventually gets ground down. To some, CMWC 2005 represented the final selling out of the messenger image. To others, it was a subtle use of cultural jujutsu where corporations were made to do the bidding of a rag tag bunch of working class punks. Who decides which is right?

The messenger community remains coherent despite being filled with antagonistic individuals, professionals, anarchists, activists, and many other cyclists who are unable to be categorized. As one messenger told me at the 2002 NACCC, "we are part of the most amazing profession with such creative, alive people who work so hard for each other and their community." I can think of no better example of this than a group of Buddhist messengers in Japan who held a Critical Mass ride to a Shinto shrine where they prayed for the safety of messengers around the world.

Messenger meetings III: Critical Mass

This Tokyo ride, a loosely organized political and communitarian action, is typical of the Critical Mass ride. More populist than an Alley Cat, and with a political edge, Critical Mass rides allow cyclists to claim the streets as their own. Cyclists in a Critical Mass ride occupy an entire street, riding together in a pack on a route decided by consensus.

Critical Mass originated in San Francisco in 1992. Over years of evolution and extension to cities around the world, it has become many things to many people. Critical Mass is simultaneously an anarchist demonstration against car culture, a celebration of the freedom of cycling, direct action against unfair laws, and, in some cases, a simple excuse to provoke drivers and cops. These many perspectives are what give Critical Mass power. The analogy to the core of atoms at the heart of a nuclear fission reaction is an apt one—enough difference collected into a small space explodes into collective action. Travis Culley (2001: 69) described a Chicago Critical Mass:

> I came upon a motley crowd. Bike messengers who looked like tired camels sat on their bikes, laughing and talking with riders dressed in suits who wore small Velcro straps around their ankles. Some guys with long beards and knitted hats wore signs with slogans like ONE LESS CAR and FUELED BY POTATOES. These greenies rode in harmony with young executives, schoolteachers, business owners, lawyers, stockbrokers. Many ages were represented. Children sat comfortably in plastic pannier seats, their round helmets tipped to one side.

People from all walks of life, who might normally disagree about politics, find themselves united around the single concept of cyclists' rights. A collection of essays celebrating the tenth anniversary of Critical

Mass rides (Carlsson 2002) shows this diversity in a dozen articles from cities across the world. Although their reasons for riding may be varied, they can all take solace in the relative safety of a mass of riders.

Just as there are different reasons for coming to the ride, there are different ideas about appropriate behavior. Some riders urge the group to violate the vehicle code by running red lights and intentionally snarling traffic while others insist on following all of the rules of the road. Some participants ride quickly, others at a parade pace. Participants occasionally come in costume, and many carry political signs. Recent political commotion in the Middle East has bred signs reading END THE OILIGARCHY and THE REVOLUTION WILL NOT BE MOTORIZED. Bicycles and riders alike are often plastered with slogans suggesting that drivers should thank the riders for being "one less car" rather than excoriate them for blocking the way. A favorite response to driver's protestations is "we aren't blocking traffic, we ARE traffic!"

Critical Mass rides are an anarchistic affair. They have no leaders and no organizers. It is a rolling form of participatory democracy. People who want to ride meet at a standard time set for their city, usually 5PM to coincide with the height of the commute traffic. Someone asks where people want to ride, a route is agreed upon, and then undertaken. There is no leader, no cadre, and the problems this poses are clear: without a central theme, without an organization, without a leader or even a spokesperson, there is little cohesion. But to many participants, the diversity of Critical Mass rides is its strength. Cyclists are forced to occupy a marginal space on a daily basis, and taking over the streets is a response to this marginalization by activists, bicycle commuters, and couriers.

Though many couriers do participate in Critical Mass, many others are highly skeptical of the rides for a variety of reasons. Some couriers call Critical Mass a ride for "tourists"—people who ride every once in awhile and think themselves superior to those who drive 100 percent of the time. One courier once liked the idea of the Critical Mass, but feels that it has become absurd:

> the first couple of years of critical mass here was cool but has slowly eroded into a joke. what started as a good idea has turned into a Disney ride for suburbanites, yuppies and bike activists with a chip on their shoulder not to mention the self righteous pc rhetoric that goes with it.

Though this is a caricature of the Critical Mass ride, the courier expressed a common feeling towards "civilian" bicycle advocates. They had their cause and did their work, but it remained irrelevant to messengers at best, and at worst, Critical Mass was a liability to the messenger community:

> ive ridden on a few and had a good time. but that has soured the last couple of years due to the fact that it affects my job and income, 1500 extra cyclists shuffling through downtown at crunch time on a busy friday and more than half of them riding like blindfolded rookies is one thing, the other is the abuse and unwarranted attention from angry commuters and police the following monday long after the massers are back in their cubicles are directed at the most visible cyclists mon-fri: us the messengers

Another messenger concurred:

> I was oft called (Mondays after CM) a "Critical Masshole" & chased a few times by irate motorists who got it backasswards. Ya know, most of the time I was honestly too wiped to ride CM & frankly dead sick of my bike by Friday, thank you. I wanted a (10) beer(s) & pizza & loudmusic, not a whole lotta yuppies on hybrids or thinking they're LeMond or whatever, egad!

The derision of some messengers towards other members of Critical Mass is understandable: messengers often feel justified in scoffing at commuters who take a self-righteous stance because they commute a few miles a day.

Other couriers take exception to this, making common cause with "Joe Public" bike rider:

> Call [critical mass] a tourist event if you will, but I think it still plays an important part in bicycle advocacy. To Joe Public, the popularity of an event indicates its social acceptance, hence creating a cultural 'bridge' between advocates on the one hand, and potential consumers of that message on the other.

Some couriers, more invested in the profitability of courier companies, also noted that the "potential consumers" of the Critical Mass "message" were also potential sources of income for bicycle messengers. Still other messengers noted that the problem was not with the messengers or Critical Mass riders, but with car culture. In fact they should be united against "autophiles" who harass cyclists:

> Some messengers say CM brings negative attention to us from police or drivers. Some civilians say our behavior brings negative attention to them from police and drivers. The problem is not CM and it's not messengers. The problem is the attitude of the police and drivers. I just don't think we should let the police and raging drivers off the hook. If CM didn't exist they would find another excuse for their behavior.

In all, messengers were mixed in their support and participation in Critical Mass rides. As one courier summed it up:

> We need the fiery ones out at the head of protests, yes. But we also
> need the ones who are out riding every day, hitting the streets on two
> wheels everyday.

In other words cycling advocates and cycle couriers both play important but different roles. Though there is significant overlap in the interests of messengers and activists, at times messengers may wear an activist hat, and at other times they may simply ride the streets as couriers without seeing their actions as political.

Critical Mass is a vibrant social movement that rationally responds to the marginalization of bicycles in the modern city. Messengers mostly support Critical Mass, though many do not participate for various reasons. Critical Mass captures the streets once each month when cyclists can ride in safe solidarity, protected from cars. Though some messengers disparage the "tourists" on Critical Mass rides, others see the rides as a gathering place for the larger bicycle community as well as a place of solace from their daily solo street riding.

Conclusion: community matters

The messenger community is both broad and inclusive, as local as it is global. While couriers can call on others in almost any large city for a couch to sleep on, they support each other locally as well:

> When I first became a messenger I was inspired by the spirit and
> generosity of messengers. My first day on the job, I got a flat. I didn't
> have a patch kit or pump and at least 3 messengers stopped to offer
> help to fix it. It was a completely different world. Strange couriers
> waved hello, and some offered advice and some concern. It didn't
> make sense in today's world. Most people seemed to actually care
> about each other. I felt like I was part of something that could teach
> the rest of the world a few lessons.

Local messengers, even from competing companies, will offer assistance, hang out on breaks together, and party at messenger-friendly bars and restaurants after work. As one courier put it, messengers have their own subculture, making them feel invincible as a community:

> There wasn't anything messengers couldn't do. We had our own
> races. We had our own 'zine. We even had our own bar and restau-
> rant.

This community is formed of the shared experiences of adversity on the job as well as the freedom that the job offers.

> We are such a diverse and incredibly awesome community of people.
> We come from all over the world, all different backgrounds, have so
> many different points of view and points of reference. We have found

common ground through a job, a lifestyle, and a serious love of a certain human-powered machine.

Despite their many differences, messengers have crafted a strong community around certain shared interests and experiences. This community is maintained and strengthened through solidarity-creating endeavors such as races and parties, but is continually under threat from co-optation.

Couriers use many forums for community building: the Alley Cat, Critical Mass rides, international championships, and after-work congregations at messenger-friendly bars. These places are safe spaces for messengers to build community by emphasizing their unique qualities to one another, focusing on common experiences, and reminding themselves of their liminal and marginal position in the streets. Informal meetings, races, and rides help socialize messengers into a community of outsiders and risk-takers. But more importantly, they offer moments where messengers are buoyed up by the energy of collective effervescence, where norms within the subculture are created and re-inscribed through contemporary rituals of solidarity.

Notes

1. Pulling is a term for what the lead rider of a pace line does. The rider in the front of the line "pulls" the others by cutting the headwind, letting those in the rear rest. The spinning of the rear wheel also creates a draft effect; when the following rider's front wheel is just a few inches away the lead rider's rear wheel generates an additional pull. It is commonly thought that such drafting techniques will save the rear riders perhaps 20 percent of their energy. Riders take turns in the front of the pace line.

2. "Skitching a ride" is when a rider grabs hold of a passing car and is towed along. This might be to help out up a hill, or to gain momentum to pass another rider. It is dangerous of course, but only in the case where a driver turns or brakes suddenly. A seasoned messenger can gauge traffic flow on the busier streets and anticipate when a driver might stop or turn. Similarly, on a hill, as traffic slows it is relatively simple to skitch a ride and get a break from pushing the pedals.

3. Few messengers from poorer nations travel to the continental championships. Though some European messengers have held races and benefits in Central America, the international travelers of the messenger community come from the global North.

4. The history of the trackstand goes back to velodrome racing. Such a race is determined almost entirely on the ability of the rider rather than strategy or wit. With well-matched racers, the main determinant of who will win is who "pulls" and who "drafts." The person "pulling" is cutting the wind or pushing the air, while the person drafting

rides directly behind the leader, enjoying a ride that saves much of their energy. The person in front thus tires more quickly, and the person behind can leap ahead just at the finish line and use her saved energy to win the race. Since the victor is determined by who crosses the line first, not how quickly the race is ridden, there is an immediate competition for who can go the slowest and thus take the drafting position, and hence the trackstand was born. It is common in one-on-one velodrome races to have the starting gun fired only to see the two riders stay totally still until one rider cannot hold it any more and pushes off into the "pulling" position. There is no logical analog to velodrome racing in the messengering industry, and so trackstands serve no real purpose. Nonetheless they symbolize a track bike rider's skill.

5. Keirin is a highly specialized form of track racing in Japan. It is a very popular gambling event, where individual riders compete in small groups. To minimize equipment advantages and maximize the chance that the result is determined only by a rider's ability, every part of the bicycle is regulated. Very few manufacturers have managed to meet the criteria of NJS, the Japanese governmental regulating body. The bikes and equipment are high quality and very expensive.

6. Conclusion: The Last Non Co-opted Punk Rock Subculture

"This is the only non co-opted, dynamic, vibrant punk rock subculture left. They tried to co-opt it but we fuckin' resisted."[1]

Living in the modern moment poses challenges to all of us. We are faced with an uncertain political, economic, and cultural terrain. Just when we think we've got a handle, it shifts underneath our feet. It often feels as if uncertainty abounds: elections are decided by courts instead of voters, corporations merge, separate, and are reconfigured under a different name. The economy rises and falls based on esoteric changes in markets across the globe, and state budget revenues rise and fall with the bumps of the economy. Oil prices skyrocket, wars rage in different nations, troubled young men go on shooting rampages. But somehow, through all this, life goes on: we wake up in the morning and make the banal everyday decisions to shower, make breakfast, go to work.

Messengers make decisions every day too. But unlike many of us, they decide every morning to get up and go to work at a very dangerous job that offers minimal wages. They make banal decisions about accepting risk almost every moment of their working day. For many messengers, this choice entails a form of economic coercion. If they don't work on the streets, they may end up living in the streets. For these couriers the job is simply a way to make a meager living. The choice to voluntarily take risks marks the messenger as belonging to a particular social group.

If they choose to, they can embrace the identity that comes with membership, but not everyone does.

Each of us creates an identity within the confines of the broader society. We do this, in part, by taking on a name. In the past, family names were often associated with the particular profession that our forefathers occupied. Now this name-taking is done out of tradition, but according to certain gender biases (we normally take the name of our fathers, but other cultures follow different rules). If our family names are tradition-bound, then our given (or "first") names offer space for more creativity. Mostly this is the decision of our parents, but sometimes we take a nick-name, and sometimes we change our names entirely. These processes of naming help us to establish an identity: I am a Smith, or a Gonzalez-Rubio, or a Gudmundsdottir. I may be Nicolas to my parents, affectionately known as Nick, but to my friends I am "The Nickster." By claiming a name we have a hook to hang our identity on.

This identity is a socially-constructed thing. Sometimes we embrace an identity that accords with norms, but sometimes we create it precisely against those norms. I might be known simply as Jim Stark to my parents and teachers, but my friends and the police know me as a leather-coated rebel without a cause. We cannot freely define ourselves, for it is up to others to accept or reject our identities based on their own perceptions. As George Herbert Mead (1934) has shown, quite often we alter our own actions based on how others perceive us, or even based on how we presume others might interpret our presentation of self. And so we label ourselves in other ways as well: we locate ourselves in our professions, in social categories, we identify with a particular group. We might be a cashier, an after-work softball player, a wife or husband, an art lover, a blogger, or a model train enthusiast. We identify with larger social groups based on similar experiences.

Sometimes this can take on an imaginary layer. We suppose that we are in some way similar to other Americans, even though it would be impossible to confirm this on an empirical level. We may assume that we are essentially similar to those who resemble us racially, or religiously, but this, too, is difficult to be sure of. There may be more similarity with some individuals across these boundaries than within them. Benedict Anderson (1991) called these "imagined communities" and we construct them through religious connection, through nationalism, but also in the way we purchase products. We live in a market society, and so we also brand ourselves through consumption: we are Coke or Pepsi drinkers.

We express our identity with the clothes we buy—FUBU or Sean John, Banana Republic or DKNY express our uniqueness. But for many this imagined community feels thin and unfulfilling. We continue to yearn for connection and search for authenticity.

Technology also has a role in how we view community and identity. Our modern telecommunication devices make interaction convenient: we can use our cell phones, email, text messaging, or Internet instant messaging to constantly communicate. But some things are lost as others are gained. Heavy Internet use can actually cause people to be more depressed, a counter-intuitive result of increased participation in the new, "virtual" communities (Kraut et al 1998, Sanders et al 2000). Cell phones allow easier connection and flexibility in meeting times and places. (I've lost count of how many times I've heard someone say "I'll call you on your cell when I get there and we'll find each other.") As a result we don't make firm plans anymore: we have become a society of cell phone flakes. But when telephones first became ubiquitous for the middle class in the post-World War II suburbs, telephone exchanges were established based on street or neighborhood names, and thus offered a sense of community and place-based identity. In the mid-1990s identification by area code became an important symbol for some New Yorkers. Manhattan's 212 area code was contrasted with Brooklyn's 718. Outer borough denizens took pride in being from "the 718" and they used this number to symbolize their identity. People went so far as to wear t-shirts and baseball caps with 718 emblazoned on them.[2] This identity separated Brooklynites from their Manhattan neighbors and defined a distinct in-group that was based on place but marked through a random technological designation. We label ourselves through inclusion in some larger set of groups, and we perform our daily lives in part according to the expectations of these groups.

Some messengers make the choice to voluntarily take risks as a way of achieving emotional fulfillment, gaining a certain form of cultural capital, and forming a distinct identity. These are "lifestyle" messengers. By actively identifying with the broader messenger culture they define their identity. They also help to construct and reconstruct that identity by performing certain behaviors that they think are appropriate for members of that group. Lifestyle messengers may ride quickly and break laws even though they are not in a rush to get anywhere, or even when they are not on the job. Though the job does not pay well financially, there are cultural and stylistic dividends—messengers get to belong to an exclusive group and feel that they are culturally rewarded based on that special status.

This subset of the larger community of couriers actively embraces the messenger lifestyle, cashing in on the popularity and attention that couriers currently enjoy. And there are many young people who want the job for the freedom it offers. There are many couriers or posengers who fit this category, meaning a large pool of labor willing to work for a small paycheck. The irony is that at the very peak moment of urban cool for messengers, innovation in information technology has reduced the actual need for couriers. This results in more workers and less work, depressing wages and creating more onerous working conditions.

To many people, couriers must seem like lunatics on wheels, running red lights and throwing themselves headlong into traffic. The riddle of why they do this is answered in part by the structure of the industry. The delivery industry leaves messengers with low pay, slight job security, and almost never any health insurance or other benefits. The piece-rate system and independent contractor status means that the more packages they carry in a day, the more cash they ride home with. So maximizing their package load means taking risks and breaking traffic laws.

But if risk-taking is in part voluntary and in part structural, then why not reduce that risk by wearing a helmet? The answer is captured by the term "the banality of risk." Risk is in the eye of the beholder: to a normal car driver or pedestrian, traffic can be unpredictable at first glance. Yet a messenger who has worked the streets long enough knows just how to look at traffic to see both the hazards and the opportunities. Part of learning the ropes in the messenger industry means understanding the unwritten rules of traffic, and armed with this knowledge messengers can navigate the streets with far less risk than uninitiated eyes might perceive. The everyday experience of this risky reality, combined with notions of the immortality of youth, and a certain elitism that comes with specialized knowledge, yields an understanding of risk as banal, almost boring. Removing the brakes from your bike raises the stakes, and makes the experience of riding the streets that much more interesting. Removing the helmet achieves the same ends: excitement and stimulation, but also the performance of risk, or style.

Beyond banality, risk is a socially-constructed phenomenon: risky behaviors are performed for an audience. In the modern moment many people feel unfulfilled and alienated by work and social life. The response to this, for some bike messengers, is to experience an emotionally charged adventure into authenticity by voluntarily taking risks. A central problem is *who* the audience is, for as with many in the service industries, a messenger is both supremely visible as a symbol of urban culture and yet the effective courier is in many ways invisible to cars. Messengers embody liminality: they are both visible and invisible. So who is the audience? All of us: the pedestrians and drivers who see or do not see the courier; commuter cyclists who may stand in awe as the courier floats an intersection; other messengers who appreciate the skill of the courier's craft.

Embracing voluntary risk and performing a messenger lifestyle can buy authenticity. Couriers look different from commuter cyclists. They act differently in traffic. When a messenger breaks normative boundaries they gain entry to courier culture. This grants authenticity and community belonging. The courier quoted earlier experienced this after his first few weeks on the job, saying, "It didn't make sense in today's world. Most people seemed to actually care about each other. I felt like I was part of something that could teach the rest of the world a few lessons." The community of messengers offers something that is in short supply in this modern world: they genuinely care about each other. In the disorienting acceleration of the current moment, when uncertainty seems the only constant, having a group to rely on is no small thing. Claiming a messenger identity allows a courier to feel at home in a heartless world.

And so the question "Why do they do it?" is much more complex than it might seem at first. The bicycle messenger industry is dominated by young men. This is in part due to the structure of the industry, and in part due to the structures of race and sex in contemporary society. Dangerous and dirty jobs are usually filled with people of color, the poor, the under-educated, or the unskilled. And many bike messengers fit this bill: in this work I call them "working messengers" to differentiate them from the more stylistically flamboyant couriers who embrace a messenger lifestyle. Many of these lifestyle messengers are young, college-educated, white men.

Why would young white men who may have other opportunities embrace messengering, and why are messengers viewed as a current icon of urban coolness? The answer comes down to the performance of risk. One courier noted that messengering "tests inherently macho insecurity" and gives young, educated, white men a way to grapple with their existential angst. Just as traditional societies tested young men, messengering allows modern males to prove themselves. The courier continued: "boys [who] want to go prove themselves as men enter the riskiest jobs they can find." Religions offer a structure for the rite of passage from adolescence to adulthood, such as baptism, bar mitzvah, or walkabout. In modern secular society this has become a matter of course, with legal definitions reducing the old rites and tests to simply surviving past the age of 18 (or perhaps 21) when full legal rights are conferred. In some secular societies this test was administered by the military, and in some nations compulsory military duty still serves this function. But today we are left without any clearly defined test to mark this important ritual passage.

The courier quoted above noted the functional role of the military for this purpose, but went on, suggesting "being a bike messenger is of course much more sexy." In many ways, young messengers are responding to the frustrations of alienation in the modern world, and they test themselves in dangerous circumstances as a way of showing their mettle. If they pass the test, they can claim a messenger identity, they become lifestyle messengers and embrace courier culture. This identity is a peg to hang the hat of one's ego upon: By claiming a messenger identity they buy status that was previously unattainable.

What status is it that these messengers are embracing? Not quite cars, not quite pedestrians, bicycle messengers occupy a complex social position, they are "somewhere in between." And yet this outsider status is what binds the community together through rituals that underscore the differences between themselves and mainstream society. Alley Cat races, messenger bars, mutual assistance organizations, and regional and global gatherings all function to define inclusion, create solidarity, and re-inscribe identity. Even though the community is diverse by race, class, gender, ability, and commitment, the messenger identity is based at least in part on shared experiences. As one courier put it, "we have found common ground through a job, a lifestyle, and a serious love of a certain human-powered machine."

This sense of community, and the authenticity of the identity behind it, is what the lifestyle messengers and posengers appear to desire. If imitation is the most sincere form of flattery, then messengers should be pleased that young people admire them so much as to mimic their dress, habits, and riding style. But of course messengers see this as a form of cultural appropriation: many couriers consider fakengers to be leeches draining messenger style of that very authenticity that attracted the posengers in the first place.

This continual threat of co-optation has lead to a diminution of messenger-chic. As one courier put it:

> I actually think that bike messengers are getting less cool; I think our
> stock is dropping. We once impressed the hipsters and squares alike
> by riding without brakes, but now they both have seen too many
> posengers crash and they think we're stupid. Everyone has had a bike
> messenger boy/girlfriend, and now they're over us and our parties,
> our dirty clothes, our sweaty smell, and our obsession with our bikes
> and our lifestyle.

This courier thinks the novelty has worn off, and the 15 minutes of fame for messengers will move on to whatever the coolseekers find next. It is an easy prediction that the sun of messenger chic will eventually set. One of the costs of co-optation is that it is short-lived. When the novelty wears off, the purveyors of mass culture will no longer pay dividends in cultural capital.

One courier from Ireland told me, in 2002, that the myriad of creative and colorful couriers constitute the last "non co-opted dynamic, vibrant punk rock subculture." This courier went on to say that "they tried to co-opt it, but we fuckin' resisted." And yet, several years later as messengers remain the urban cool "flavor of the month," the issue of co-optation still rages as posengers cash in on the messenger identity and the issue of selling out dominates much of the community's conversations.

While no one is really in favor of selling out, the resistance this courier described is being worn away. Yet the punk rock and DIY spirit of the messenger community makes it difficult for a full exploitation of the messenger image. After years of resistance, many couriers argue that the messenger scene was sold out in New York City in the summer of 2005. Others suggest that this was a subtle harnessing of capitalism by those who saw an opportunity to make "the man" work for them, for once.

So bike messengers ride a fine line. They use a narrow slice of the street to expedite the flow of business. And while this supports the capitalist system, it also enables an existence on the edge as an outsider. At that edge, riding that line, messengers can live a life of their own choosing: floating through traffic thinking that they can see around corners, racing with comrades in Alley Cats, or parading in a Critical Mass. Though many messengers ride eight hours a day and go home to their families, the profession also enables a DIY life of anti-hierarchical self-organization where messengers can find community with those who share their chosen identity.

Many of the contradictions and complexities of modern life are reflected through the struggles of bike messengers. We desire to stand out amongst the uniformity of modern life, negotiating our identities by embracing names and labels. In contemporary market society our identities are wrapped up in and expressed by the products we consume. Dinner is McDonald's or Burger King because there is not enough time to cook for ourselves. We wear FUBU or DKNY to express our originality and uniqueness, but the obvious, if banal, contradiction is that millions of people are all buying the same clothes to express their individuality: we are all choosing from the same menu. This is an expression of social power. Though considering ourselves unique individuals acting with free will, the reality is that we present ourselves to one another largely by way of choosing from that same menu. Henry Ford once quipped about his mass-marketed Model T, that "a customer can have it painted any color he wants so long as it is black." Uncritical or unconscious choices help to reproduce the illusion that capitalism offers a singular freedom, when in fact what it offers is a set of improvisational moves within a strict context—we can express ourselves, but only through the act of purchasing and consumption, we can choose any job we can get, but are forced to work for wages. Each of us balance being workers, family members, consumers, and members of a larger community. We tiptoe through the intricate politics of race, class, gender, and hierarchies of power. And the navigation of these complexities plays out in our lives under capitalism, representational government, and the pressures of finding fulfillment within a system that produces a seemingly inevitable alienation.

Messengers have a unique set of complexities to navigate: the balance between buying in and selling out, wanting to exist as an outsider but threatened with co-optation, the struggle of making a living in an exploitative economic system, the contradiction of an alternative lifestyle and radical politics faced with the reality of greasing the wheels of commerce. The vibrant culture that messengers developed helps to solve some of these problems by highlighting an authentic identity, building a community of solidarity, and valorizing risk, skill, and creativity. Yet these unique complexities resonate with many of our everyday choices, and indeed they reflect those very same systems of power that we all struggle with daily. Perhaps the solutions that messengers have found can teach all of us some lessons.

Notes

1. A Messenger from Dublin, Ireland interviewed at NACCC in Houston, 2002.

2. As Manhattanites moved to the outer boroughs in search of lower rent or a bigger yard or the sense of community that neighborhoods offer, gentrification ensued. Hip hop artist 2 Skinny J commented on this in his 1998 song called *718*: "I spent my rent so I road train coaches / Across the bridges to emigrate / from 212 to 718."

Methodological Appendix

This book started innocently enough. I worked as a bicycle messenger for several years in a capitol city in the northern Midwest. Partially this was just for fun: I was a graduate student, working on my Masters and Doctorate, and I needed some distraction. But as a teaching assistant my wages were meager, and messengering helped to pay bills. Over time, I came to realize that my participation was not just fun and distraction, but that I was being an ethnographer without realizing it—an accidental ethnographer. As many sociologists will testify, once you come to look at the world through a sociological lens, it becomes difficult to turn that off. What I saw amazed me, and I wanted to look more carefully. This was the moment of engaging the sociological imagination, when the citizen's perspective moves to the background, and the sociologist moves up to the front. It is an example of what some people call "the sociologist at work," that is, the moment when sociological insight can situate the particular within its general context.

In this work I strived to achieve what Dorothy Smith calls institutional ethnography (Smith 2005). Through this approach to participant observation work, the social scientist moves from empirical data collection to show the lines of power that lace through social life. This work is similar, too, to Michael Burawoy's extended case method (Burawoy 1991), with some critical distinctions. Burawoy argues that the extended case method is to be differentiated from the two classical approaches to participant observation: ethnomethodology and grounded theory. Criticizing ethnomethodology for reducing all sociology to the micro, and grounded theory for reducing all sociology to the macro, Burawoy argues that the extended case method seeks a "genetic strategy" rather than a "generic" one, a strategy of explanation that offers "historically specific causality" which can allow the reconstruction of theory. Burawoy does not want to take social structures as a "given" as he argues that the symbolic interaction tradition does. Instead, he asserts, the extended case method "seeks to uncover the macro foundations of a micro-sociology" by contextualizing the empirical social situation into "given general concepts and laws about states, economies, legal orders, and the like to understand how those micro situations are shaped by wider structures" (Burawoy 1991: 280-82). But what are these "given" structures, if not what those symbolic interactionists assume? Burawoy suggests that the extended case method allows a connection between the micro and the macro, where the micro informs the reconstruction of our understanding of the macro. But how the researcher makes these connections is somewhat mysterious, and the examples Burawoy offers center on rebellion and resistance.

Dorothy Smith (2005) gives us another approach, what she calls "a sociology for people," the logical outgrowth of her "sociology for women" (Smith 1987). Though at first blush, institutional ethnography sounds similar to Burawoy's method, it is in fact a radical departure from traditional sociology—Smith herself calls it a paradigm shift. The concept of institutional ethnography also starts with the micro, but by explicitly setting it in the context of "ruling relations." A sociology for people begins from the actions of our everyday world and "explores social relations" which are "not fully visible to us." It is a method of inquiry that produces knowledge, but rather than starting from established (and ossified) theoretical positions, instead "starts from the actualities of people's everyday lives" in order to discover the organization of the social and "explicate or map that organization beyond the local of the everyday." This is not some rarified knowledge, but rather a "means of expanding people's own knowledge rather than substituting the expert's knowledge for our own" (Smith 2005: 1, 10-11). Thus, contrary to Burawoy's macro foundations of micro-sociology, the objects of study are not objects at all, but people and their actions, and how these exist in, produce, and reproduce a network of ruling relations. This stands in stark contrast to traditional sociology, where scientists observe subjects and produce abstract generalizations.

Instead of taking structures or macro levels for granted, Smith argues that we must explore how these are instantiated on the ground and built up through people's everyday lives. In some ways, she follows Marx's assertion that we make history, but not under circumstances of our own choosing. We act, and in doing so we produce and reproduce the varying norms, conceptions, and relations of the world. The existence of those norms cannot be taken for granted, but rather bear exploration. How the macro forces of political economy shape the lives and thoughts of people cannot be assumed *a priori*—in fact the very objectified notion of "political economy" must be problematized. Instead the connections need to be traced out in everyday life. Smith suggests that institutional ethnography can make explicit the connections that remain implicit in Burawoy's method by extending "ethnography beyond the locally observable" to show how "translocal forms of co-ordinating people's work . . . are to be found in the actual ways in which co-ordination is locally accomplished" (Smith 2005: 37-8).

And so this participant observation study started innocently enough. I was immersed in the everyday social action of messengers, and connected deeply with this social group, their style, cognitive perceptions of the world, and subculture. Through this process, I came to see the bike messenger industry as a problematic: a terrain to be discovered and explored. Over more than five years I participated in the many different activities of this community: messenger races, national gatherings, and Critical Mass demonstrations, but most importantly I worked day-in and day-out (in between teaching and going to class and doing research), performing the daily grind of delivering parcels by bicycle to clients all over the city. These experiences form the core of data for this book: the gatherings and races allowed me to observe both individuals and the broader group dynamics under diverse circumstances, and the daily work of being a messenger allowed me to fully immerse myself in the rough and tumble work of riding the streets. It is this daily experience that brings the most intimate level of understanding for an ethnographic work. From that standpoint, I have attempted to trace the lines of power that connect to the less visible ruling relations.

The job of the participant-observer is a difficult one. You must at once be part of the group, but also be thinking more abstractly outside of the current moment. Taking notes at the odd spare moment and more carefully after work means that some details are left out, or slightly altered by one's own deceptive memory. This, of course, is inherent in the social science process—unlike a chemist or biologist, the sociologist's laboratory is the messy social world, a place without controls where experiments cannot occur in a beaker or a petri dish. The data that results from the participant observation method however, can give rich detail to the particular case being examined. For this book I carried out hundreds of individual interviews with messengers and friends, both on and off the record. On occasion I would ask messengers questions under the guise of the social scientist. But mostly we would just be sitting in a bar, congregating at a break time, or riding around town. Though its difficult to characterize some of these as "interviews," I did ask pointed and probing questions at times to try and draw out answers to particular research questions.

Beyond individual interviews, I also had many group conversations at gatherings of all sorts, from messenger parties, to Critical Mass demonstrations, to the regional, national, and international championships. Participating in large social occasions allowed me to watch what people were doing, how they were interacting, what sorts of postures or identities they seemed to be presenting, and how these varied in different situations. Particularly interesting in this regard was the set of interactions between messengers and non-messengers who were just along for the ride, folks who are sometimes called "citizens," as well as non-messengers who looked the part of a messenger, sometimes called posengers. These interactions provided insight into how messengers behaved with out-group members. On occasion, I would follow up by asking how messengers, citizens, and posengers experienced those situations.

Much of the data comes also from an international electronic-mail discussion forum, where messengers discuss anything and everything. There are several hundred participants from around the world on this forum, and discussions generally take place in English—there is clearly a selection process by language and class (owning or using a computer and email system), and a self-selection process for participation. Debates range from the appropriate terminology for certain types of bikes, to what prizes should be given for what types of races, to which city is hardest to work in. An ever-recurring debate was "brakes or no brakes" on fixed gear bikes as well as discussion about posengers and corporations.

I have also drawn information from three popular-press accounts of messengering, as well as from newspaper and magazine articles where messengers were quoted. I benefited from the work of some messengers in establishing the "Messenger Institute for Media Accuracy" which collects and posts news stories on a website. News media reports on messengers are remarkably consistent in their comments on the various stereotypes of messengers mentioned in this text—sweaty, grimy, and distinctively stylish young white men who flout traffic laws. That these couriers make up perhaps only 10 or 15 percent of messengers never seems to occur to these reporters, perhaps because the other 85 percent remain ubiquitously invisible.

Throughout this work I quoted messengers precisely as they spoke or wrote, without editing for grammar, spelling, or punctuation. This means that all slang, spelling or grammatical errors, and obscenities originate with the person quoted. I hope that this gives the reader an understanding of messengers' communication style. Many of these quotes show the depth of feeling about their experiences. It poses an interesting problem to the ethnographer: do you correct someone's spelling when quoting from an email posting to a discussion forum? Or do you offer ellipses to take out the "ums" and "uhs" that form normal conversation? I have chosen not to, again in order to describe in the most rich detail how messengers communicate with themselves and others.

To preserve the confidentiality of those I spoke with, I used no real names or identifiable nicknames (excepting those named in published sources). In cases where labels were necessary, I gave couriers pseudonyms that seemed to conform to the intent of their often-colorful names.

There is very little social science research on bicycle messengers. I hope that this ethnography offers a foundation for further inquiry and useful research on these flamboyant individuals and exciting subculture. I do not claim that I have been able to cover everything about this group, but I highlighted what I see as the most important aspects, and situated them in theoretical, historical, and social context. As with any ethnographic examination of a particular case, I cannot claim scientific objectivity, nor can I argue for external validity of this work. But I do argue that this work is objective in the sense of my deep understanding and participation in the community, combined with subsequent external analysis and reflection. Practitioners of participant observation methods can, in mimicking positivism, strive for generalizability and objectivity, but as with all social sciences it is impossible to know everything at once. There is no Archimedean point from which the scientist can observe the social world. All we can do is immerse ourselves and examine the nitty-gritty of social life, and then extricate ourselves to re-examine the data, connecting the dots and tracing the lines of power.

References

Abbott, Andrew. 1991. "History and Sociology: The Lost Synthesis." *Social Science History* 15(2): 201-38

American Civil Liberties Union (David A. Harris). 1999. *Special Report: Driving While Black.* http://www.aclu.org/racialjustice/racialprofiling/15912pub19990607.html.

Anderson, Benedict. 1991. *Imagined Communities.* London: Verso Press.

Arendt, Hannah. 1963 *Eichmann in Jerusalem: A report on the banality of evil.* New York: Penguin.

Attewell RG, Glase K, McFadden M. 2001. "Bicycle helmet efficacy: a meta-analysis." *Accident Analysis and Prevention.* 33(3): 345-52.

Baker, Alan J. 2005. "Bike messengers lose business, not hope: Digital age changes messengers' role; e-mail and faxes cut carrying load." The Colombia *Chronicle.* 31 May 2005.

Bakunin, Mikhail. 1971. *On Anarchism.* Edited and translated by Sam Dolgoff. New York: Black Rose Books.

Baxandall, Rosalyn and Linda Gordon. 1995. *America's Working Women: A documentary from 1600 to the present.* New York: Norton.

Beck, Ulrich. 1992. *The Risk Society: Towards a new modernity.* London: Sage.

Bellah, Robert, Richard Madsen, William M Sullivan, Ann Swidler, and Stephen M. Tipton. 1985. *Habits of the Heart: Individualism and Commitment in American Life.* New York: Harper and Row.

Berger, Peter L. 1963. *An Invitation to Sociology: A Humanistic Perspective.* Garden City, NY: Anchor Books, Doubleday.

Bettis, Pamela J. 1996. "Urban Students, Liminality, and the Postindustrial Context." *Sociology of Education.* 69(April): 105-125.

Block, Fred. 1990. *Postindustrial Possibilities.* Berkeley: University of California Press.

Borkowski Press Centre. 2004. http://www.borkowski.co.uk/archives/press/2004_01 .html.

Boskin, Michael J., Ellen R. Dulberger, Robert J. Gordon. Zvi Griliches, and Dale W. Jorgenson. 1998. "Consumer Prices, the Consumer Price Index, and the Cost of Living." *The Journal of Economic Perspectives* 12(1): 3-26.

Bourdieu, Pierre. 1977. *Outline of a Theory of Practice.* Cambridge: Cambridge University Press.

———— 1984. *Distinction: A Social Critique of the Judgment of Taste*. Cambridge: Harvard University Press.

Boyle, Philip J. 2004. "Mapping the Lines: An Exploration of Mobility and Urban Spaces Amongst Bicycle Couriers." Masters of Arts Thesis, University of Windsor, Department of Sociology and Anthropology. Windsor, Ontario.

Brooks, David. 2000. *Bobos in Paradise: The new upper class and how they got there*. New York: Simon and Schuster.

Burris, Beverly. 1998 "Technology and Work Organization." *Annual Review of Sociology* 24: 141-57.

Braverman, Harry. 1974. *Labor and Monopoly Capital: The Degradation of Work in the Twentieth Century*. New York: Monthly Review Press.

Burawoy, Michael. 1982. *Manufacturing Consent: Changes in the Labor Process under Monopoly Capitalism*. Chicago: University of Chicago Press.

Burawoy, Michael, Alice Burton, Ann Arnett Ferguson, Kathryn J. fox, Joshua Gamson, Nadine Gartrell, Leslie Hurst, Charles Kurzman, Leslie Salzinger, Josepha Schiffman, and Shiori Ui. 1991. *Ethnography Unbound: Power and resistance in the modern metropolis*. Berkeley: University of California Press.

Calhoun, Craig. 1996. "Rise and Domestication of Historical Sociology." Pages 305-37 in *The Historic Turn in the Human Sciences*, edited by Terrence J. McDonald. Ann Arbor: University of Michigan Press.

———— 1998. "Explanation in Historical Sociology: Narrative, General Theory, and Historically Specific Theory" *American Journal of Sociology* 104(3): 846-71.

Cockerham, William. 2006. *Society of Risk-Takers: Living life on the edge*. New York: Worth Publishers

Culley, Travis Hugh. 2001. *The Immortal Class: Bicycle Messengers and the Cult of Human Power*. New York: Villard.

Curtis, Kim. 1998. "Bicycle Messengers Might Unionize." The Associated Press. 9 December 1998

Dennerlein, Jack and John D. Meeker. 2002. "Occupational Injuries Among Boston Bicycle Messengers." *American Journal of Industrial Medicine* 42: 519-25

Douglas, Mary 1992. *Risk and Blame: Essays in cultural theory*. London: Routledge.

Durkheim, Emile. 1995 [1912]. *The Elementary Forms of the Religious Life*. (Trans. Karen Fields) New York: The Free Press.

———— 1984 [1893]. *The Division of Labor in Society*. (Trans. W.D. Wells) New York: The Free Press.

Dworin Caroline H. "Wings on their heels." *The New York Times* 14 November 2008.

Elias, Norbert. 1982 [1939] *The Civilizing Process*. Oxford: Basil Blackwell.

Errington, Frederick. 1990. "The Rock Creek Rodeo: Excess and Constraint in Men's Lives." *American Ethnologist*. (17)4: 628-645.

Ferrell, Jeff. 2005. "The Only Possible Adventure: Edgework and Anarchy" in Lyng, Stephen (ed.) *Edgework: The Sociology of Risk Taking*. New York: Routledge.

Foucault, Michel. 1979. *Discipline and Punish: The Birth of the Prison*. (Trans. Alan Sheridan). New York: Vintage Books.

———— 1980. *The History of Sexuality, Vol. 1*. (Trans. Alan Sheridan). New York: Vintage Books.

Freeman, Aaron. 2004. National Public Radio's *All Things Considered*, 3 May 2004 "Commentary: Bicycle Thieves' Essential Role" http://www.npr.org/features/feature.php?wfld=1869196

Giddens, Anthony. 2000. *Runaway World.* New York: Routledge.

Gilbert, Jess and Kevin Wehr. 2003. "Dairy industrialization in the first place: Urbanization, immigration, and political economy in Los Angeles County, 1920-1970." *Rural Sociology.* 68(4): 467-490.

Gutsche, Robert Jr. 2003. "Messenger troubles afoot: Business slides as clients adopt Net technology." The Chicago *Tribune.* 13 October 2003.

Haber, Samuel. 1964. *Efficiency and Uplift; Scientific Management in the Progressive Era, 1890-1920.* Chicago: University of Chicago Press.

Hall, Carl T. 1992. "Workers' Comp Costs Throwing Bike Messengers Out of Work." The San Francisco *Chronicle.* Page A1. 8 January 1992.

Hansen KS, Engesaeter LB, Viste A. 2003. "Protective effect of different types of bicycle helmets." *Traffic Injury Prevention.* 4(4): 285-90.

Hari, Johann. 2005. "Death Wish: Shocking Increases in Promiscuity and a culture of high-risk sex." *The Independent.* 7 November 2005 Features Section. London: Newspaper Publishing PLC.

Harvey, David. 1982. *The Limits to Capital.* London: Basil Blackwell.

———— 1989. *The Condition of Postmodernity: An enquiry into the origins of cultural change.* London: Basil Blackwell.

———— 1996. *Justice, Nature, and the Politics of Difference.* London: Basil Blackwell.

———— 2000. *Spaces of Hope.* Berkeley: University of California Press.

Harris, Kathleen Mullan, Greg Duncan, and Johanne Boisjoly. 2002 "Evaluating the Role of 'Nothing to Lose' Attitudes on Risky Behavior in Adolescence." *Social Forces* 80: 1005-1039.

Hausman, Jerry. 1999. "Cellular Telephone, New Products, and the CPI." *Journal of Business & Economic Statistics* 17(2): 188-194.

Hebdige, Dick. 1980. *Subculture: The Meaning of Style.* London: Methuen.

Hobsbawn, Eric J. 1996a. *The Age of Revolution: 1789-1848.* New York: Vintage Books.

———— 1996b. *Age of Extremes: 1914-1991.* New York: Vintage Books.

Holyfield, Lori and Lilian Jonas. 2003. "From River God to Research Grunt: Identity, Emotions, and the River Guide." *Symbolic Interaction.* 26(2): 285-306.

Hoover, Ken. 1999. "Bike Messengers At S.F. Company Vote to Join ILWU." San Francisco *Chronicle.* 2 June 1999.

Kidder, Jeffrey L. 2005. "Style and Action: A Decoding of Bicycle Messenger Symbols." *Journal of Contemporary Ethnography.* 34 (3): 344-367.

———— 2006. "'It's the Job that I Love': Bike Messengers and Edgework." *Sociological Forum* 21(1): 31-54.

Kilgannon, Corey. 2005. "Bike Messengers Take the Street to the Track." *The New York Times* 10 June 2005.

King, Anthony. 1997. "The Postmodernity of Football Hooliganism." *The British Journal of Sociology.* 48(4): 576-593

King, Mike and Nicolas Van Praet. 1994. "Bike couriers want to unionize." The Montreal *Gazette,* 2 April 2004.

Kraut, Robert, J. Patterson, V. Lundmark, S. Kiesler, T. Mukopadhyay, and W. Scherlis. 1998. "Internet Paradox: A social technology that reduces social involvement and psychological well-being?" *American Psychologist.* 53(9): 1017-1031.

Kropotkin, Peter. 2002. *Anarchism: A Collection of Revolutionary Writings.* New York: Dover Publications.

Lasch, Christopher. 1978. *The Culture of Narcissism.* New York: Norton.

Laurendreau, Jason. 2006. "'He Didn't go in Doing a Skydive': Sustaining the Illusion of Control in an Edgework Activity." *Sociological Perspectives* 49(4): 583-605.

Lears, T. J. Jackson. 1981. *No Place of Grace: Antimodernism and the transformation of American culture, 1880-1920*. New York: Pantheon.

Lemert, Charles. 2005. *Social Things: An Introduction to the Sociological Life*. New York: Rowman and Littlefield.

Levy, Frank and Peter Temin. 2007. "Inequality and Institutions in 20th Century America." Working Paper. Cambridge: MIT Industrial Performance Center.

Li G. and S.P. Baker. 1997. "Injuries to bicyclists in Wuhan, People's Republic of China." *American Journal of Public Health* 87(6): 1049-52.

Liebowitz, Stan and Stephen E. Margolis. 1995, "Path Dependence, Lock-in, and History." *Journal of Law, Economics, & Organization*. 11(1): 205-226.

Liker, Haddad, and Karlan. "Perspectives on Technology and Work Organization." *Annual Review of Sociology* 25: 575-96.

Lois, Jennifer. *Heroic Efforts: The emotional culture of search and rescue volunteers*. 2003. New York: NYU press

Lotchin, Roger. 1991. *Fortress California: 1910-1961 from warfare to welfare*. New York: Oxford University Press.

Lupton, Deborah. 1999. *Risk and Sociocultural Theory: New Directions and Perspectives*. New York: Cambridge University Press.

Lyng, Stephen. 1990. "Edgework: A Social Psychological Analysis of Voluntary Risk-Taking." *American Journal of Sociology* 95(4): 851-86.

——— (ed). 2005. *Edgework: The Sociology of Risk Taking*. New York: Routledge.

Marcus, Greil. 1990. *Lipstick Traces: A Secret History of the Twentieth Century*. Cambridge: Harvard University Press.

Marx, Karl. 1967 [1867]. *Capital: A Critique of Political Economy, Volume I: The Process of Capitalist Production*. New York: International Publishers.

McShane, Larry. 1992. "Economic Cycle Flattens Life for NYC Bicycle Messengers. The Boston *Globe*. 6 May 1992.

Mead, George Herbert. 1934. *Mind, Self, and Society*. Edited by Charles W. Morris. Chicago: University of Chicago Press.

Mernin, Brendan. 1996. "A Story about New York Bicycle Messengers." *Bicycle Trader*. 13 (September).

Mills, C. Wright. 1951. *White Collar: The American middle classes*. Oxford: Oxford University Press.

——— 1959. *The Sociological Imagination*. Oxford: Oxford University Press.

Mohammed, Michael. 2002. "Study Finds Work Risk Great for Bicycle Couriers." *The Harvard Crimson*. 26 November 2002.

Mol, Artur and Gert Spaargaren. 1993. "Environment, modernity and the risk-society: The apocalyptic horizon of environmental reform." *International Sociology* 8 (4): 431-459.

Mol, Artur. 2002. "Ecological modernization and the global economy." *Global Environmental Politics*. 2(2): 92-115.

U.S. Department of Health And Human Services, Centers for Disease Control and Prevention, National Center for Health Statistics (NCHS). 2002. *Health U.S*. Washington D.C.: Government Printing Office.

Nietzsche, Friedrich. 1978 [1885]. *Thus Spoke Zarathustra, A Book for All and None*. Translated by Walter A. Kaufmann. New York: Penguin.

———— 1977. *The Portable Nietzsche*. Edited and Translated by Walter A. Kaufmann. New York: Penguin.

Noakes, T.D. 1995. "Fatal Cycling Injuries." *Sports Medicine.* 20(5): 348-62.

O'Hara, Craig. 1999. *The Philosophy of Punk: More Than Noise*. San Francisco: AK Press.

Palmer, Catherine. 2002. "'Shit Happens': the selling of risk in extreme sport—Interlaken and Everest tourist tragedies." *Australian Journal of Anthropology.* December 2002.

Piore, Michael and Charles Sable. 1984. *The Second Industrial Divide*. New York: Basic Books.

Proudhon, Pierre-Joseph. 2003 [1851]. *The General Idea of the Revolution in the Nineteenth Century*. New York: Dover Publications reissue of Beverly Johnson (ed.) 1923 version published by Freedom Press, London.

Riley, Rebecca "Lambchop." 2000. *Nerves of Steel*. Buffalo: Spoke and Word Press.

Rodgers, Gregory B. 1996. "Bicyclist Risks and Helmet Usage Patterns: An Analysis of Compensatory Behavior in a Risky Recreational Activity." *Managerial and Decision Economics.* 17(5): 493-507.

Sanders, Christopher E., Tiffany Field, Miguel Diego and Michele Kaplan. 2000. "The Relationship of Internet Use to Depression and Social Isolation among Adolescents." *Adolescence.* 35(138): 237-42.

Schumpeter, Joseph A. 1938. *The Theory of Economic Development: An Inquiry into Profit, Capital, Credit, Interest, and the Business Cycle*. Cambridge: Harvard University Press.

Scott, Joan W. and Louise Tilly. 1989. *Women, Work, and Family*. New York: Routledge.

Shaiken, H. 1984. *Work Transformed*. New York: Holt, Rinehart and Winston.

Shapiro, Isaac and Robert Greenstein. "Trends in the Distribution of After-Tax Income: An Analysis of Congressional Budget Office Data." *Center on Budget and Policy Priorities Bulletin.* Washington, DC: Center on Budget and Policy Priorities.

Sivak, M, DJ Weintraub, and M. Flannagan. 1991. "Nonstop flying is safer than driving." *Risk Analysis* 11 (1): 145-148.

Smith, Dennis. 1991. *Historical Sociology*. Philadelphia: Temple University Press.

Smith, Dorothy. 1987. *The Everyday World as Problematic: A feminist sociology*. Boston: Northeastern University Press.

———— 2005. *Institutional Ethnography: A Sociology for People*. Toronto: AltaMira Press.

Staff writer. 2003. "Bike messenger rides through hazards of the job." The Edmonton *Examiner* 15 October 2003.

Staff writer. 2005. "Don't kill the bike messenger." *The New York Times.* 11 June 2005.

Staff writer. 2007. "Bike Messengers – A Vanishing Breed?" *Messenger Courier World Magazine.* Winter.

Steffensmeier, Darrel and Emilie Anderson Allan. 1995. "Age Inequality and Property Crime: The effects of age-linked stratification and status-attainment processes on patterns of criminality across the life course" in John Hagan and Ruth D. Peterson (eds.) *Crime and Inequality*. Stanford University Press: Palo Alto.

Talese, Gay. 1959. "Messenger Boys Fading Away: The Alger Hero Disappears Unlamented As Western Union Modernizes; Electronic Speed Wins; Facsimile Reproduction and Phone Telegrams Take Toll of Puttee Corps." *The New York Times.* 2 December 1959.

Tilly, Charles. 1981. *As Sociology Meets History*. Orlando: Academic Press Inc.

———— 1984. *Big Structures, Large Processes, Huge Comparisons*. New York: Russell Sage Foundation.

Tomasson, Robert E. "Fax Displacing Manhattan Bike Couriers." *The New York Times*. 19 March 1991.

Turner, Victor. 1967. *The Forest of Symbols: Aspects of Ndembu Ritual*. Ithaca: Cornell University Press.

———— 1974. *Dramas, Fields, and Metaphors: Symbolic Action in Human Society*. Ithaca: Cornell University Press.

———— 1982. *From Ritual to Theatre: The Human Seriousness of Play*. New York: Performing Arts Journal Publications.

U.S. Census Bureau. 2006. *Current Population Survey*. Annual Social and Economic Supplement, Series PINC-05. Washington D.C.: Government Printing Office.

van Gennep, Arnold. 1960 [1908]. *The Rites of Passage*. Chicago: University of Chicago Press.

Vidal, Matt and Matt Zeidenberg. 2007. "Average Wage, Family Income, and GDP Productivity." Working Paper. Madison: Center on Wisconsin Strategy.

Weber, Max. 1958 [1905]. *The Protest Ethic and the Spirit of Capitalism*. New York: Scribner.

———— 1946. *From Max Weber: Essays in Sociology*. Translated and edited by Hans H. Gerth and C. Wright Mills. Oxford: Oxford University Press.

Wehr, Kevin. 2004. *America's Fight Over Water: The environmental and political effects of large-scale water systems*. New York: Routledge.

Weyland, Jocko. 2007. "Unstoppable." *The New York Times*. 29 April 2007. Accompanying Internet photo and audio slide show at http://www.nytimes.com/2007/04/29/nyregion/thecity/29gear.htm.

Whitesnake, Josh. 2007. "A Reason I Work on a Road Bike." www.messNYC.org

Index